Breaking Free

The Death of Her Brother Sends a Woman in
Search of His Killers and Her Identity

Pamela Penrose

BookPartners, Inc.
Wilsonville, Oregon

BookPartners, Inc.
P.O. Box 922
Wilsonville, Oregon 97070

Author's note: I wish to assure the reader that while names and places have been changed in this story, the events related are true and have not been exaggerated or blown up to make them more sensational which seems to be the trend today. As a result, I think you will find the sinister forces described in this book more real and threatening.

Pamela Penrose

This book is written and dedicated to my brother Mike. My investigation of his life and his death led me to delve into myself and seek the meaning of my own life which resulted in changing it. I honor him for his struggles and his failures which so tragically ended his life.

Acknowledgements

I want to thank my family and friends who stood by me even when they didn't understand what I was doing. I also want to acknowledge my publisher who translated my story into a coherent whole that adheres to the events as I lived them. Without their belief in me this book could not have become a reality.

My early life had been fed with dreams and a deep feeling that if I waited, did my part and was patient, love would come to me and with it such a family life as fiction depicted and romance built up. It seems to me that I have always been waiting for something better — sometimes to see the best I had snatched from me.

Quoted in "Dorothy Mendenhall:
'Childbirth Is Not a Disease'"
By Gena Corea, Ms., April 1974

Table of Contents

Chapter One

It was a nightmare that drove me out of my bed at the State Line Motel in northern Idaho. I fought the tangled, clutching sheets as if they were part of the evil in my mind. On weakened legs, I stumbled to the light switch that turned on the floor lamp in the corner of the room near the single window and unfastened the chain guard on the door. I threw it open, then slammed it shut behind me as I stepped out on the sidewalk that fronted the long row of adjoining motel rooms.

I had learned long ago that taking deep breaths helped banish my fear and quiet my thumping heart. So I gulped the air as if it would fill me with courage. Even for late August, it was cold outside and a chilling breeze from the nearby Snake River raised goose bumps on my arms and legs. I was standing in the dark in my thin, cotton nightgown that reached to just above my knees. I could see the night light through the motel rental office window.

There also was a floodlight that threw a yellow circle on the paved entrance driveway to the motel. I was grateful for the pale illumination, a sign that I was not alone.

I hate bad dreams. Oh, God I hate them! For the first twenty-one years of my life, I was afraid to go to bed; I fought sleep until my eyes betrayed me and I awoke later with a muffled scream in my throat I was unable to utter.

Now after years of reprieve, here I was shivering and frightened of my old enemy, the dark. My nightmares had always been violent and the one I had just escaped from was no exception. I shuddered as I remembered seeing my brother, Mike, who lived in Texas, laying on his stomach in the middle of a dirt road. There was a red-haired man perched on Mike's back with one knee pinning Mike flat on the ground. The man was bent forward over Mike's head, pushing his face and mouth into the dirt with his hands. His eyes were slits in his face and his expression was cruel and intent, reflecting his murderous frame of mind.

At first, I wondered why Mike wasn't fighting back. He was a tough muscular man, a fighter who never took a back seat to anyone. That's when I realized Mike was drugged. I didn't know how I knew that was true, but, as with many of my nightmares, along with the paralyzing fear, I was endowed with a certain prescience that gave me the ability to understand more of what was happening in a dream than I could see. There could be no reason for Mike not to struggle with the man unless he was incapacitated from some drug he'd been given.

Even with his face mashed into the dirt, his mouth rimmed with dust, I could see tears running down one side of Mike's face. As my heart hammered with terror for him, in the same moment I felt deep sorrow and an infinite sadness over the ending I knew was going to happen to

Mike.

It seemed predictable that Mike's assailant suddenly shifted one restraining hand from my brother's face and drew a plastic bag from his back pocket. I wanted to scream at Mike, "Wake up! Hurry, wake up!" But my warning never left my frozen tongue and I watched Mike's killer pull the clear plastic bag over his head and twist the open end in a tight knot around Mike's neck.

I saw Mike's face turn red, his mouth pop open and shut like a fish drowning in an ocean of air. I tried to look away, tried to avert my eyes, but I was horror stricken. My gaze fixed on Mike's purpling lips, as his feeble movements grew weaker and he died. With a final convulsion, his tongue protruded from his swollen lips like a sullen rebuke of his killer.

When Mike quit struggling, his red-haired killer released his grip on the knotted end of the plastic bag and pushed himself off of Mike's back. Then he turned his wicked eyes and stared at me contemptuously. He looked into my soul and smirked when he saw me shrink and shiver like the coward I felt myself to be.

I stood with my bare feet drawing cold from the cement sidewalk in front of my room a few minutes longer, then remembered a little poem I memorized when I was twelve, desperate with the nightmares that haunted my sleep.

I never knew who wrote it, but I used to say it to myself as if it were a token or charm that would protect me from the hateful dramas that formed like blood clots in my sleeping mind. It was never a cheerful poem, but somehow it gave me a little strength, like a perverse saying has a sort of authority of its own that makes it stand out.

In the sinister dread of dark,
all the dogs of nightmare bark,
and I, wounded, terrified mind, must wait,
helpless victim of blood and hate.

I knew I would never go back to sleep with Mike's murder dream so fresh in my mind. I determined to get in my car and drive toward home, stopping at the first all night restaurant that could give me coffee. As I threw my clothes and toiletries into my bag, careful to leave the door to my room wide open, I decided I would call Mike in Chilton, Texas first thing in the morning to make certain that my nightmare had not been a premonition that turned out to be true.

The aftermath of nightmare was always the same. From the time I was a kid jumping out of my bed, pursued by demons and grotesque phantoms, I ran for my life to outdistance them. Often I plunged out of my house and flew down the center of the deserted nighttime street.

In the open I felt less vulnerable. Sometimes, when I was far enough away from my bedroom to feel safe, I sat quietly on other people's porches or under street lamps until, inevitably, my mom, urged awake by that mysterious maternal sense of awareness which warns mothers of their children at risk, came along and took me home.

Always, I spent the remainder of the night on the living room couch in the company of the T.V., falling into an exhausted sleep with the comforting sound of human voices coming from the flickering screen.

I got behind the wheel of my van after dropping my bag on the rear seat and swung onto the access road that eventually would lead me to Interstate 84. That was the fast highway bordering the Columbia River into Portland. It was a great drive almost any time of the year. High summer was the best, of course, when the broad river descended west like a contented smile through craggy mountains. The wind, often playful, often strong enough the shake the world, rode up the Columbia River gorge, battering trees, churning white caps, and washing the air blue with brilliance.

It was a five hour drive from where I started in Idaho to Gresham, Oregon, a Portland bedroom community. It was where I lived when I wasn't on the road selling welding supplies.

The house in Gresham was a tri-level in which Tom, my husband, who was a brakeman for the Union Pacific Railroad, my two sons, daughter and stepson, and I lived. Adam was the oldest, then came Nathan, four, and the baby of the family, Kathleen. Jesse, Tom's son by a previous marriage, completed the circle.

As for Tom and me, we lived in a state of unarmed hostility. We had reached that point at which warring couples stay together because of the common bond that unites them — their children. It is never a good excuse for the failure of two humans to make peace with their mistakes and give each other the freedom of a separate, better life. Also I believe that in a disintegrating marriage both partners are deeply resentful of the idea that his or her spouse can be happier with somebody else. The kids, often, are used as innocent hostages of their parent's feelings of hurt and anger.

"If I can't be happy, you can't be happy either. The kids are your responsibility as much as mine." That's the refrain that married couples use to defend their pride and wound their spouses. No vulgarity, or smart-alec humor, or overstatement, can ever extinguish the guilt for the marriage disaster each spouse must bear. To admit cooperation in defeat would mean that both partners must take equal blame for the failure.

I drove for an hour before I found an all-night café open where I could fill my thermos with coffee. As I left the diner, I caught a glimpse of myself reflected from the polished surface of the tall coffee urn.

Dear God, I thought, I looked like the Wreck of the Hesperus. I have long, dark red hair and it was uncombed. There was a snaggle of strands sitting on the top of my head like a dark red mouse. The little makeup I wore had vanished and my face was pale, making my dark brown eyes with fatigue bruises under them seem to pop out of my head.

With my disorganized mop of hair, stark expression, wrinkled blouse and the ratty sweater I always put on to drive, I must have made a great impression on the tired waitress who poured coffee for me and took my money. No wonder she looked at me strangely.

I have never been a pretty woman, but I've been told there is a sparkle and confidence in me that gives my face a lift, an attractiveness and a complimentary sharpness. I think people like me because I'm basically honest, like to laugh, and get excited about ideas. I know I'm determined, trusting, and don't like to be hurt. On the whole, I guess, as I drove to Portland, sipping hot black coffee, I was Mrs. Average American woman and that, I said to myself, is quite a lot.

It was three-thirty in the morning when I stopped at the diner. I decided I would call Mike at his home in Chilton, Texas about four-thirty my time, which meant another hour of driving. Texas was two hours later, so Mike would be having his breakfast.

All of us in my father's family were early risers and

Mike, who was an auto mechanic for WalMart Monday through Friday, got to his job about seven-thirty. On weekends, he worked for himself doing engine tune-ups and other mechanical jobs on automobiles.

I was only sixty miles from Portland when I pulled over the second time and found a phone booth near a Chevron station — too early for it to be open — in Hood River.

Of course, I was still haunted by a residue of fear from the dream I had of Mike being suffocated. I wanted to hear his voice before I could bury my apprehension.

When I heard him at the Texas end of the line, my heart lifted.

"Mike, is that you?"

"Yes, Sis? Where are you calling from?"

"From Oregon. I had to call to be sure you are all right. One of those crazy nightmares of mine. In it you were…hurt."

I decided on a white lie because I was a little embarrassed about dreaming him dead. Also I didn't want to give him a reason to worry.

"I thought you'd grown out of those nightmares," he said.

"This is the first one I've had since I was twenty-one. It was probably just a fluke, but I had to call and find out if you were all right. You are all right, aren't you?"

"Sure, Sis, I'm fine. I'm glad you called though. It was thoughtful."

We visited a few minutes longer, compared notes on family members and how they were doing. We chatted about a family reunion and where it might be held, then Mike said he had to leave for work, but would I be home to take a call from him after he got off work? He wanted me to give him instructions on how to weld a cast-iron manifold on an old Caterpillar tractor.

When I replaced the receiver on the payphone, the new day was beginning to show its colors, a soft rose blush dawning east on the Columbia, spreading slowly into the dark that blanketed the width of the great waterway.

For a moment I thought about Mike's request for information on welding the old cat, and I remembered the hours and days and months I apprenticed with my dad, a master welder who had perfected his skill far above the mark of craftsmanship into an art. I was the oldest of his children and it was me he chose to become the receptacle of his knowledge. I was pleased as punch, because I loved and respected my father, except for his drinking and the violence that came out in him when the booze ignited his temper. Always, my mom caught the brunt of his alcoholic rage.

But as a master welder, my father had no rivals. And when he was sober and in his teaching mood, he was kind and gentle. Not only did I learn about welding, but he taught me about metals, their intrinsic strengths and weaknesses and the bonding materials and techniques to use to make them adhere in a strong union.

One day, something I'll never forget happened in his welding shed near the back of the house when we lived in Artesia, California. We had been talking about the tricky composition required to make a sincere weld, when he turned directly to me, brushed his hands together as if to signify the end of something and said, "Well, you've got a brain like sticky paper and you don't mind telling people your opinion. When we started out, I had an idea that you might take to welding like a bear to honey. Now, you've got a real trade. Don't let the fact that you're a woman stop you. My craft is mostly practiced by men. When you look for jobs, you're going to be laughed at and they'll poke fun at you. It's up to you to prove how good you are. They'll swallow their jokes and jibes when they see you perform."

He gave me a big hug, which in a way was my graduation present from my dad's private one-student school of welding theory and application.

It was my four-year-old, Nathan, who next saw Mike, and what he said about his uncle frightened me because his words proved to be true a day later.

When I arrived home from my trip to Idaho, Tom had just completed his graveyard shift as a brakeman in the Portland freight yards and was in the kitchen. He greeted me perfunctorily, finished his breakfast egg sandwich, left his dishes and the frying pan for me to clean up and sauntered off to bed.

I was relieved that I didn't have to talk to him. As for the kids, it was still school vacation time and as often as possible during the week after my return from Idaho, I took them on excursions and picnics and outings, and scheduled my sales calls appropriately.

My conversations with Tom, when we were civil enough to talk to one another, never touched on the real issues that divided us. We lived in a small, artificial world in which violence was always threatening like a storm on the horizon, and the kids and I walked on eggs to avoid provoking Tom into an explosion.

Saturday night, September 4, I had just settled down in my bed when I heard Nathan scream. I jumped up, followed by my Labrador, Red, and rushed to Nathan's room. When I pushed the door open, I noticed the fur around Red's neck, actually all over his body, standing on end. He looked like a ferocious bristle brush.

Nathan threw himself in my arms, then pointed in the direction of the living room downstairs. His body was shaking and there were tears in his eyes when he said, "Mom, Uncle Mike's in the living room. He's crying. His face is all scrunched up. He needs us real bad. We've got to help him."

I'd never seen Nathan so disturbed. I tried to calm him, convince him that his uncle was in Texas. He couldn't be in the living room.

"No," he cried, shaking his head stubbornly. "I know he's down there. He needs us. You've got to go."

I gave Nathan another hug and assured him I would go downstairs and look for Mike. Nathan wanted to stay in his room, so I told him I'd be right back and headed down the hall. Red followed me, but only as far as the landing at the top of the stairs. There he stood growling, his fur stiff and bristly.

I thought Red was acting strangely, but I couldn't put a reason to his behavior. Of course there was no sign of Mike on the first floor. When I told Nathan, he frowned and acted as if he didn't believe me.

"I know he was there, Mom. Maybe he left."

I coaxed Nathan back to his bed and rubbed his back until he relaxed. I explained softly that everybody had bad dreams and once in a while the dreams pictured loved ones as being hurt and they called on us for help. "They seem awfully real," I told him.

Eventually, Nathan fell asleep, but I knew I had not convinced him that his dream did not portray reality. Red curled up near Nathan and his fur subsided as I soothed my son.

When I returned to my own bedroom with Red at my heels, grateful that the other kids had not been awakened by

the commotion, I was tempted to call Mike, but I decided
against it. It was one a.m. in Oregon, three a.m. in Texas. I'd
wake him out of a sound sleep with my son's dream as my
only excuse. Also, though I had not shared my own
nightmare with Nathan, I had already talked with Mike, first
from the pay telephone in Hood River, and then again a few
hours later when I answered my brother's questions about
the welding project he had.

As I put out the lamp on my bedstand table, I
wondered about little Nathan. Was he to be disturbed, like I
was for years, by strange and violent dreams that had made
me flee my bed in terror, but whose gory content never
came true? I hoped with all my heart that he would not be
another victim. The years had harder tasks ahead for him,
for every one of us, than to be burdened with the frightening
appearance of nocturnal monsters that thrilled and smirked
and flashed their claws and teeth in fanciful imitation of
murder.

I soon discovered how badly I had misjudged the deep
meaning in Nathan's dream. The following afternoon my
father called from Texas. Mike was dead. He'd been found
hanging from a rope attached to the long arm of a cherry
picker. The police were calling his death suicide.

When I told Nathan and the other children of their
uncle's death, Nathan pinned me with his eyes, full of accusation and hurt.

"I told you," he screamed. "I told you he needed help.
But you wouldn't listen. You didn't believe me."

For the rest of that terrible day, Nathan avoided me,
refusing to speak to me or acknowledge my presence when
I tried to console him.

I think that day was the saddest one of my life. I
understood the deep meaning that came into my mind as I

suddenly remembered words that I had forgotten long ago from a Thornton Wilder play we studied in high school. It was *Our Town* and what he wrote was:

"That was what it was to be alive. To move about in a cloud of ignorance; to go up and down trampling on the feelings of those about you. To spend and waste time as though you had a million years...."

To move about in a cloud of ignorance! That was me. I was ashamed of my lack of insight and my failure to honor my son's premonition. One certainty was clear to me. I knew in my heart that Mike had not committed suicide.

Chapter Two

I had cried over Mike's death about as much as I was going to. Tears have no place, I decided, in a heart that has turned to stone. And mine seemed frozen. After I had accepted that he was dead and listened to my father's scathing opinion of the police verdict of suicide, my heart had seemed to grow a hard shell.

My mind cleared and one thought came to dominate my life and plan my direction: after the funeral in Texas I would stay on in Chilton and find out who killed my brother and why. I didn't even stop to consider how preposterous, and perhaps dangerous, such a course of action might be. I didn't think of myself as a small, inept woman, certainly with no training in police investigative techniques or even in simple methods of interrogation.

I was so angry, so caught up in a terrible sense of outrage and loss, that I turned cold and hard. I'd always reacted to injustnice, unfairness or harm in this way —

taking the hurt inside and surrounding it with a tight knot of soreness, like flesh building scar tissue around a thorn that has pierced it.

Though separated by sex and size and mentality, Mike and I, from the time we were children, had shared a strong similarity in the way we viewed people and life. He was like an alter ego to me and I knew I would feel his absence in my heart with a bitter, unstoppable determination to investigate his death.

I knew better than to tell Tom about my decision to investigate Mike's death. When I informed him of what had happened to my brother and that I was going to Texas for the funeral, he made a crack that even for him was vicious and overwhelmingly stupid. It revealed how warped and bitter he was.

"I'm not surprised you're going. Mike never did like me. He probably died just to give you an excuse to leave me and go to his funeral."

I was dumfounded. God, what a fool! At that moment, I despised him with a deep and grainy hate more satisfying than the waves of rage that had swept over me when he abused me with his foul mouth or threatened to strike me.

I turned my back on him and walked into my bedroom to pack for Texas. I was shaking like a leaf.

Five days later, after leaving the children at my sister's house in Anaheim, California, I drove into Chilton, Texas. As I guided my van through the main paved streets, with signs of the early September heat in the wilted, dusty trees, and in the stifling, sticky stillness, too hot and oppressive to encourage movement, I felt my hostility rise. I had entered enemy territory. There were parked cars gleaming in the brightness, glare shields propped on the dashes to protect against sun damage. Present were the inevitable pickups with gun racks supporting polished rifles, the drivers with straw cowboy hats pulled low, wearing dark sunglasses to protect against the blazing sky.

Central Texas had always given me the impression of closed communities with guarded secrets, whose residents lived by a surviving primitive code upon which the superficial world of commerce (cattle, oil, agriculture, tourism) was superimposed like oil on water. I knew such an estimation was probably unfair of me, but my frame of mind was clouded by anger, and the deep wound in my heart brought on a strong desire in me to weep every time I thought about Mike hanging from the arm of a cherry picker.

I knew my brother better than any human who had entered my life, and his essential nature, even had he been terribly depressed, would have prevented him from killing himself. There were no circumstances I could ever imagine that would have driven him to suicide.

As I drove to the funeral home where Mike's body lay after getting directions at a service station, I was honest enough to admit to myself that at this stage of my grief everybody in this southwest town of burning air and sun-browned grass was guilty of conspiracy in Mike's death. I had no desire to be charitable or generous in my views. I was on a manhunt for the killers of my baby brother and there was no room in my empty heart for sentiment or fairness, and surely there was none for any touch of doubt about the righteousness of my course.

I greeted my mom and dad in the chapel at Simpson's Funeral Home and Mortuary. God bless them, they had survived almost thirty years of my father's drunken temper and wildness when he was boozed up, and his infidelities when the alcohol triggered his sexual drives. Then they were divorced. Dad lived in Texas and Mom in California near two of my sisters. As I took in my mother's face, the lines of resignation and self-effacing timidity were there for anyone to see, and I wanted to hold her in my arms until all the memories of insults and bruises, and shame for betraying herself, went away.

But I loved my dad; sober he was kind, helpful, a tower of strength. When he hugged you, you knew he would never let anything bad happen to you. Now, standing a little bowed in his six-foot-two stature, there was anger and bewilderment in his eyes.

He put his arm over my shoulder, and with my mom trailing on the other side of him, he led me through the surprisingly large crowd of sisters, brothers, cousins, nieces, aunts and uncles and friends of Mike, to my brother's open casket.

Of course, Mike didn't look natural. Even the cosmetic art of the best mortician cannot erase the last subtle expression of surprise and sorrow on the face of the dead. Maybe it was just my imagination, but in Mike's face I detected reluctance and a residual anger.

I turned away quickly; I didn't want to seal my final memory of my brother with a parting vision of him that described the last act of final loneliness.

As we turned away, grief like a curtain of rain graying Mom's face, my father said in a low, fierce voice of anguish and disgust, "Mike didn't kill himself. No one in this room believes that, no matter what the goddam police say."

I accepted Dad's verdict without comment. I couldn't ignore my relatives any longer, however, and for the next half hour or so, I visited with them individually. I don't think one of them failed to say, "You really don't believe Mike killed himself, do you?"

As I moved around the chapel greeting my family and

Mike's friends, many of whom I did not know, the general mood of bewilderment and disbelief was an angry undertone in the room. I was gratified and encouraged by that buzzing hostility and found myself impatient to get through the funeral customs and the graveyard service. Mike was dead. Lingering over the last rites merely delayed my pursuit of truth, and I had little patience with them. I had said my private goodbye to my baby brother three thousand miles away, before I started the long journey to find his killers.

I sighed with relief when Mike's coffin was ritually lowered into the parched Texas soil and the Methodist preacher, from the local church of the same denomination infrequently visited by Mike, closed the service, blessed my parents and left them with well-meant, but inadequate comfort words.

When I told my father of my plans to uncover the facts concerning Mike's death, he didn't seem the least bit surprised. After the service, the two of us sat together for coffee and pie in a refrigerated restaurant a few miles from the cemetery where we had buried Mike. With two of my sisters, Mom had elected to go to their hotel, to rest and grieve in solitude. The funeral for her youngest son had exhausted her. She needed refuge, and consolation from her daughters.

"What's your first step?" Dad asked me.

"Talk to you," I replied. "You told me you were at Mike's house before the cops cut him down from the hanging rope."

"Goddam bastards," he said, laying his fork next to his half eaten apple pie. "They left him hanging, sort of half suspended, like a bent paper clip, for nearly five hours while they ransacked his house. They must have gone through every inch of it."

"But how come they left him with the rope around his neck? That was disrespectful and insensitive! Did you ask them to cut him down?"

"You bet. Sons of bitches! One cop just looked at me with frosty eyes and said, " You may be his father, but this is a crime scene, even if it is suicide. We've got our investigation to do, and our methods. We'll get to him when we're ready. The best thing for you to do is to go on home until we notify you."

"'I'll wait,' I told him. He just shrugged and walked away."

My dad explained that he had lounged in his car for almost six hours while the police conducted their investigation, leaving only for coffee now and then and a toilet break. Mike was finally disengaged from the rope after the long interval, then sealed in a plastic body bag, and carted away in an ambulance. I'll never forget the sudden blaze in my father's eyes, the hardening of his jaw and the straight uncompromising line of his lips pressed together, when he leaned across the table, covered my right hand with his calloused palm, squeezed and said in a gritty voice, "Pam, I saw Mike's neck when they let him down. Even from where I stood just behind the yellow crime tape they had strung around the front yard, the house and garage, I could see there was hardly any bruising on his neck. That's one thing. The other is, though he had grown stiff and his legs were bent in about a thirty degree angle, the vertical distance from the outright arm of the cherry picker where the rope was attached to the ground was less than six feet. Mike was six-two, the same height as me. How in the hell do you hang yourself — the idea is to break your neck from the fall — when the distance to the ground is less than you are high?

"Don't forget, the whole principle of hanging is to drop far enough for the weight of your body against the rope to snap your vertebrae. When that happens, the flesh around the circle of the rope is broken and bruised. Even if the neck doesn't break and the person strangles, there's going to be a lot of damage to the skin and muscles. Can't be helped. But Mike's neck wasn't bruised from what I could see. To make sure, I talked to the mortician at Simpson's Funeral Home. He seemed more than a little bit uncomfortable when I asked him about the bruising. His answer was wishy-washy. He said, like he wished I'd go away, that sometimes bruising is light. It all depends. He avoided giving me a direct, honest answer.

"The police are incompetent! And so is the coroner who showed up. He wagged his head solemnly and said, yep, suicide, clear as day. Later, some local judge came along, pursed her mouth and said, 'It is an obvious case of suicide.' I just couldn't believe what I saw and heard. I think there's a conspiracy going on, but I don't know why. Maybe you can find out."

My father sighed wearily, wiped his mouth with his paper napkin, and pushed away from the table. He stood up, put both hands on my shoulders and looked me squarely in the eyes.

"Be careful, Sis," he said. "This is a foreign country. I don't like the feeling I get from the cops here. They're hiding something, and they don't try very hard to disguise it. You'd better be on your tiptoes."

He turned to go, hesitated, then stepped back, bent over so his mouth was close to my ear. I could smell the coffee on his breath and the strong maleness of this man whose scent I remembered with fondness and pride from the days he was my teacher, tutor and critic when I was a teenager in his work shed with a welding torch in my hand applying what he had so earnestly taught me. I felt a pang of warmth in my heart for him when he whispered, "I've just lost a son. I don't want to lose a daughter. Be careful! Keep your eyes open, and your ears tuned for warnings. You're smart, but I've got a hunch maybe you are wading into something a lot deeper than we both know. Good luck and keep me posted. I'll come running if you need me."

As my father climbed into his car and headed home to Gunbarrel, an hour and a half away, I remembered a statement John Webb, my brother's close friend and neighbor, had made to me earlier at the chapel. Added to what my father had just said to me, it was pretty evident that my own suspicions about a conspiracy surrounding Mike's killing were far more substantial than guesswork. My next move, I decided on the spur of the moment, was to drive to John's house and ask him to describe what he had found in Mike's backyard six days ago when Mike's son had banged on his front door. Hysterical, his eyes streaming tears and his elevated voice stuttering with fright, he had managed to cry out, "Dad — Oh, please help. He's hanging in the garage!"

Earlier, when John Webb and I stood together in the chapel, he said to me he believed the cops were dirty, somehow indirectly involved in Mike's death through their connection with the person or persons who had killed Mike and arranged his body to look as if he had hanged himself.

Of course, he said, proving it was another matter, but maybe the first step was for me to corner Mike's sixteen-year-old son, Matt, who was whacked out of his head on drugs most of the time. Where did the kid get his supply?

Talk to the kid, he advised, if I could get him sober

long enough to make sense. One thing for sure was that the boy was scared to death of the cops. He was on probation for drug use.

When the boy was questioned by his grandfather about the events of the night before he found his father in the garage, Matt had been evasive, whining that he had been asleep and knew nothing about what happened until he started looking for Mike the next morning and discovered him hanging from the cherry picker he used to hoist engines from autos for repair work.

John had snorted in disgust.

"Damn little liar. I don't know why Mike put up with his son sniffing coke up his nose, skipping school, telling his dad fairy tales that the kids he ran with at school had a small supply. Bullshit! That kid has a habit bigger than an occasional fix.

"Also, he should get his lies straight. He told Sarah, my wife, before the police came — I told you they took their own sweet time — that from his bedroom he heard noises down below around midnight, he thought. He said he didn't pay much attention because his dad didn't keep regular hours, and often he was in the garage at odd times. He was sure he heard the ladder Mike kept on a hook in the garage fall and bang against the side of the house."

John and I were interrupted before he could finish his line of thought. Later, at the graveside, except for his harangue against the Chilton cops for their cynicism and crudity by leaving Mike's body hanging for five hours, John was morbid and sad. He never got back to his theory.

But now, as I stepped into my van and sat behind the wheel for a minute, I speculated that John's idea of police connivance in the murder made more than common sense. It would account for their hard nosed attitude, and their insistence that Mike's death was suicide. If they supported a homicide theory, that would mean an official investigation into Mike's death. And that was the last thing the cops wanted. Everything my dad had told me and John Webb had elaborated on seemed to point to police involvement in my brother's murder. At the very least, it pointed to the notion that the cops were covering up...because they were involved, getting paid off, to assure the security of the blanket of silence that protected the local drug organization?

It was a fascinating question that grew bigger in my mind the more I thought about it. It had terrifying implications for me. For if it was true, and if my nosing around and suspicions opened the wrong doors, then it seemed pretty logical that I could become the next live target. Who was there to protect me if the cops were a part of the conspiracy that killed Mike? Sure, I could call on my dad, but he was two hours away, and besides, he didn't have any local influence. Basically, I was on my own, alone and undefended.

All of a sudden, I realized how completely vulnerable I was, how simple it would be for me to meet with a convenient accident. I took a deep breath and decided I would have to find some method to protect myself, to put me at arm's length from the police and from Mike's killers, whoever they were.

It dawned on me how it might be done, and I put the idea in the back of my mind to let it grow and mature.

It was time for me to visit John Webb at his house and get his firsthand description of how he had found Mike, examined the death scene, and arrived at his own verdict about the circumstances of his friend's death before he called the police.

After visiting with John, my next move, I decided as I

put my van into gear, would be to perform the task I dreaded: making a detailed, room by room tour of my dead brother's house.

John's house was a structural twin to Mike's, the same white-painted wooden two-story, except that compared to my brother's neglected home, John's place was clear and bright, the postage-stamp yard green with healthy grass and decorative borders of snapdragons and daisies that followed the gracious curve of the small lawn.

Mike's house, with its bare front yard, sidewalks and concrete pathway leading to the front door steps sprouting sparse tufts of yellowing grass in the cracks, looked desolate, old and uncared for. The front screen door leaned away from the door frame and there were long scratches in the wire mesh. The windowpanes were dusty and the drapes that fell beside the windows on the inside hung unevenly. There were large bald spots on the hard-packed earth in the remaining patches of lawn struggling to survive without water and care.

As I took in Mike's deteriorating house, I shook my head. I remembered his writing to me five years earlier and sending a glossy postcard picture of his new home. He, his wife Dawn-Lee, and their son Matt, eleven, posed proudly in front of their new house with smiles to match the bright green manicured lawn that lay in the foreground of the snapshot.

I gave my dog Red a good hug, reminded him to stay in the van with his water bowl and cracked the window to give him air. I slammed the door behind me as I stepped out. I felt a lump in my throat as I walked up the pathway to John's front door, averting my eyes from the shabby signs of failure next door. What in the world had happened to Mike? I wondered. How had he lost his pride, his sense of respectability, his private virtue and initiative as a man? The evidence of his decline, of a shadow over his heart, made me a little sick to my stomach and depressed.

Sarah, John's petite brunette wife, a compact, pretty woman in her late thirties just beginning to accumulate life lines beneath her blue eyes, flung open the screen door for me and demanded firmly, "How are you holding up?" She took my hands in hers and squeezed. I smiled at her, feeling as though the effort had cracked my lips.

Just then John Webb came into the living room and Sarah adjourned to the kitchen to pour coffee for the three of us. When we were settled in the living room, John said, "I'm glad you came, Pam. I think it's important for you to know the details of the day I found Mike after Matt burst through the front door crying, incoherent and hysterical about his dad.

"There's absolutely no question in my mind that too many things don't add up for Mike's death to be called suicide. You already know my feeling about that. I told you at the chapel that I didn't trust the cops. You'll understand why when I describe what I found six days ago when I ran next door. It seems much longer than that, so much has happened."

John explained that he bolted out of the front door while Sarah comforted Matt and almost tripped when he crossed his lawn, then skidded on a patch of loose gravel in the driveway leading to Mike's garage. He lost his footing, but recovered before he fell to his knees. He opened the wooden gate suspended between the six-foot gap that separated the left front corner of the house from the right-hand corner of the garage. Countless was the number of times since he bought the house next door that he had pushed open the swinging gate to enter Mike's backyard.

The squeaking protest of the hinges never failed to irritate him as he passed through. On several occasions he had accepted Mike's careless invitation to oil the bleating hinges, and though he quieted the aching shriek, he was always reminded of the complaint, as the gate swished shut like a quiet rebuke behind him.

But on that terrible Friday morning, bent on verifying his friend's death, John halted inside the gate, stunned into immobility by the tableau on the cement slab extension of the garage floor. The wide side doors of the garage were flung open, revealing machine tools, mechanical equipment, a large hydraulic jack, and hand tools resting in leather holders that lined the walls in rows above a long work bench.

Standing upright in the shadowed interior of the garage, but partially exposed to the blazing sunshine, was an awkward steel sentinel with a horizontal arm. It was the bright orange cherry picker Mike used to hoist and suspend engines ready for removal from autos. Hanging by a clothesline rope tied to the horizontal arm was Mike Penrose, his face pointed downward as if in a final act of contrition and prayer. His chin rested on his chest. Around his neck, above the collar of his blue work shirt, was the other end of the clothesline — drawn up under the shelf of his chin, then angling upward in a sharply vertical direction.

John Webb, devout Christian, companion to Mike in the work they performed at WalMart, a man who deeply cherished his friendship with his neighbor, was awed and pained by the sight of his beer buddy and confidant. It wasn't right that Mike should be dead in such a crude and…uncomplimentary fashion. It was a gross contradiction to the way he lived, to his happy goodnight airs, the optimistic joy with which he greeted each new day. Yes, hanging was uncomplimentary to Mike, the word that best described the awkward final pose of the man John had admired. Despite his shortcomings and his heavy drinking, which had made him do foolish and stupid things during the last few months of his life, Mike had never borrowed trouble or invited an evil fate by apprehending it, though he had been warned. There was something very wrong about Mike's death and John knew it.

Damn, he swore to himself and moved a step or two closer to examine the confusing posture of the silent figure. John couldn't quite decide what troubled him until he realized that by his estimate the sagging body was elevated about three feet from the cement floor in a posture that was semi parallel to it. And that didn't make any sense. It seemed to rule out suicide. John backed off a few feet, then scrutinized Mike carefully. The greatest vertical distance of the body from the floor, he concluded, was at the point of Mike's rear pockets. The downward angle of his pose decreased sharply as it reached his cowboy boots. The heels of his boots supported the bulk of Mike's weight, John guessed.

The longer he stared at Mike, the more convinced John became that his friend had been propped by other hands into the position he occupied. Somebody had gone to a lot of trouble to pose him so that at first glance it appeared as if his body had slipped down from its first vertical position to the slouching partially horizontal angle it now occupied.

Bastards! John cursed beneath his breath. The whole setup might have passed the inspection of a casual witness if the onlooker didn't stop to consider one crucial fact. And you didn't need a measuring tape to confirm it if you had sharp eyes. The distance from the horizontal arm of the cherry picker, on which the upper end of the rope was tied, to the cement floor was exactly six feet.

Anybody who had taken the trouble could have discovered that Mike was six-feet-two-inches tall. A man can't hang himself by the standard method if he is taller than the distance he's got to fall for the rope to break his neck!

With a sudden step forward, John reached out with his fingers and gently pulled down on the rope circling Mike's neck. He did not exert enough pressure to disturb the position of Mike's head. As expected, John found the crease the rope made in the flesh was not deep; it was pink, not red or purple. Most revealing of all, as John examined Mike from both sides, peering closely at the skin, he detected the complete absence of any bruising. Mike had not hanged himself, he had died some other way. After killing him, somebody had rigged him up to resemble a hanged man. But they'd been in too much of a hurry to do the job right.

Turning on his heel suddenly, John rushed from the garage, and sprinted across the lawn to his front door. He learned quickly from Sarah that she had convinced Matt to take a nap. He was knocked out, snoring quietly in their bedroom. Oblivion might help to restore his shattered nerves, she observed.

John grabbed his camera from the hall closet, commenting to his perplexed wife, "I'll explain when I get back." Then he ran out the front door. When he had taken photos of his silent friend, exhausting the entire fresh roll of film in his camera, he let his arm drop with the camera dangling from his fingers.

Then, in a quiet voice, he said as if Mike were not in a state beyond understanding, "I don't know what you did to deserve what they did to you, but I've got a record on film now of how you look. I've got a hunch it may come in handy."

John Webb turned away from his dead friend, hesitated, fastened his eyes once more briefly in sorrow on the still crumpled figure as a final farewell, then opened the gate between the house and the garage. As he passed through, he remembered a verse from Ecclesiastes:

> *The almond tree shall flourish,*
> *and the grasshopper shall be a burden,*
> *and desire shall fail;*
> *because man goeth to his long home,*
> *and the mourners go about the streets.*

John's story had started fresh tears in my eyes and I dabbed at them with a kleenex. I was grateful beyond words to this kindly man, about the same age as Mike had been, a friend who had proved his loyalty to my brother far beyond the definition of ordinary friendship. His admiration for Mike had not faltered when he abused himself with drink. Also, I was certain that Mike had thoughtlessly slighted, insulted, or provoked John in ways that no doubt would have ended the relationship for a less devoted friend.

"Thanks for everything you've done, John," I said.

I hesitated, then asked, "I'd like to see the photos you took in the garage, even though I know they're terrible. Do you have them here?"

Obligingly, John rose to his feet and disappeared into a room down the hall.

When he returned, he handed me an undeveloped spool of film, and said, "This is yours. I didn't have prints made on purpose. There's nobody I know here in town who I could trust to keep their silence when they saw what was on the pictures. If the police learned about the film, they'd probably confiscate it. The film proves that Mike didn't kill himself. You'd have to have a compelling reason to suppress that fact in order to stick with a suicide verdict. The Chilton cops may have such a reason."

As I got behind the wheel of my van, grateful beyond my ability to express for the friendship and courage of John and Sarah Webb, I gave my dog Red a strong hug when he greeted me with lavish affection. I realized as I started the motor that John had given me not only proof of Mike's murder, but the power to protect myself from the cops and their allies should they decide my enquiries were bringing me too close to the truth about Mike's death.

Earlier I had decided to write a letter addressed to the FBI in Dallas, Texas, explaining my suspicions about Mike's faked suicide and the tie-in I believed existed between the cops and my brother's killers. I was going to send the letter to my dad in Gunbarrel with instructions that it was not to be opened except upon notice of my death. I knew the idea sounded Hollywoodish, melodramatic, strictly the kind of defensive ploy movie writers would plot into a script. I had to remind myself that I was up to my ears in dangerous undercurrents, treachery and threats of violence of which I had glimpsed only the surface signs.

I was like a pilotless ship threading an uncharted course through a wretched sea populated by invisible submarine icebergs whose sharp edges could flay and sink me.

Of course, my defensive hand was strengthened by the roll of film John had given me. When I wrote the letter for the FBI, I would include it in the same envelope with the description of its significance. I accomplished that chore in my motel room, then drove to the main post office in

Chilton where I purchased a small, sturdy envelope and a larger one. On the small one I wrote the address of the FBI in Dallas I had looked up, and in it I sealed my handwritten letter and the unopened roll of film. I placed appropriate postage on the envelope and put it in the second envelope with a note of instruction to my father. Then, finally, I paid a post office counter clerk the fee to send the larger envelope to Gunbarrel by registered mail.

Convinced I had done as much as possible to protect myself, I drove to the County Courthouse in downtown Chilton. There I was to meet the female judge who had appeared at the scene of Mike's death along with the county coroner.

My meeting with Judge Justine Perkins in her chambers was the final step in my plan to subtly warn an influential member of the Chilton Police and Justice hierarchy that if harm came to me while I was in Chilton asking questions about my brother, then my death would trigger a letter with instructions and Chilton authorities would have to cope with an investigation from which it was doubtful they could emerge without public exposure and criminal punishment.

Judge Perkins's secretary pointed me to a chair in the judge's anteroom and I waited for five minutes. Then I got to my feet and said firmly to the woman whose desk nameplate identified her as Noreen, "I have a four o'clock appointment with Judge Perkins. Call her and tell her I'm here or I'll leave and discover later if she encourages her receptionist to keep visitors waiting." The woman's eyes widened; she started to protest, then with a flounce turned in her chair and announced me to Judge Perkins.

The blond, slender woman with the silver-rimmed

glasses perched on her thin, aquiline nose, who sat behind a massive walnut desk, smiled politely when I introduced myself. But she did not rise to greet me. She examined a sheet of paper on her desk and, raising her peach-brown eyebrows in a question mark, said, "You're the sister of the man who committed suicide, is that right?"

"Yes, but he didn't commit suicide."

"Oh? My information is that the coroner's verdict was that Mike Penrose took his own life."

"Judge, his death is why I'm here. I intend to prove he was murdered."

She frowned, creating an unbecoming nest of tiny wrinkles between her eyebrows. "How do you propose to do that when the police have already closed the case?"

"It may not be easy, but I intend to follow my nose wherever it leads me."

"Miss Penrose, my advice to you is to go back home. Leave the police work to those who are qualified to do it. I realize it may be difficult for you to accept that your brother hanged himself. But when people are depressed and increase it with alcohol, my experience is that they often do things they would never do in their right mind.

"Also, I should give you a friendly warning, a caution really, that you can get into unexpected trouble by following your nose, as you put it into areas that are sensitive and best left alone."

"That's the real reason I asked for an appointment, Judge. I plan to go ahead, dig and poke around, ask questions, until I discover the real the truth about my brother's death. That may seem foolish to you, but I'm going to proceed. I thought I'd explain that if I am harmed, or threatened, a letter I've written will be mailed to authorities who have a wider jurisdiction than the Chilton police."

The frown on Judge Perkins face deepened as she weighed my words, then said carefully, "Ordinary people hide all sorts of secrets, Miss Penrose. They can ascribe your probing to other motives that might compromise them, and that can get you in trouble. Accidents do happen, you know."

I rose from my chair, smiled pleasantly at her and said, "I wrote the letter I described to forestall any accidents. I hope things work out that way."

As I placed my hand on the bronze doorknob to let myself out, I turned slightly toward her and observed, "I don't think the police can ever justify ignoring facts or evidence they disagree with."

Chapter Three

I'm not sure I believe in ghosts, but the day after my visit to Judge Justine Perkins, when I went to Mike's house looking, for what I wasn't certain, I had the uncomfortable, apprehensive feeling of being followed. The skin on the back of my neck bristled, and several times I was irresistibly forced to whirl around quickly where I was standing. Of course, nothing was there to greet me. As I walked the cluttered rooms and halls of the house left in shameful disarray by the careless police, I was subdued by the oppressive atmosphere and I stopped frequently, slowing my breath and pulse and listening. I swore I could hear whispering, nibbling little sounds like mice chattering over morsels of hard cheese. It was disconcerting.

I thought it was my imagination, but my common sense convinced me that perhaps places where violence had occurred retained the raw memories like weak, restless energy. It must be discharged somehow and maybe it came out in closets, walls, floors and stairs as creakings, subtle movements and low rustlings. I was particularly disturbed by soft scrapings, as if someone were desperately scratching with short fingernails on a windowpane.

I thought about occupying a bed in Mike's house and discarded the idea. I could not imagine waking alone where death had so recently come, and where it lingered like a palpable shadow. Even with Mike's friend John Webb living next door I didn't feel safe. I should have felt secure with John so close by. He had proved to me that his friendship with Mike lasted past the grave when he gave me the roll of film he had taken a few minutes after he found my brother.

I think John blamed himself for being negligent about not investigating Mike's house when he first thought something was wrong. He said he had heard noises but had decided that Mike had finally come home and was in his garage tinkering. An auto mechanic, Mike worked on weekends repairing cars or doing tune ups. It was a steady source of extra income.

The day of the funeral, John came up to me after Mike was interred and said self-consciously in a soft, troubled voice, "I feel like a shit for not going over to Mike's house earlier. I had a hunch there was something wrong. I felt uneasy, but couldn't put my finger on why. When I found him in the garage strung up to the cherry picker, I just fell apart. I couldn't believe my eyes. I knew he was dead the minute I saw him, but I didn't want to believe it. Maybe, if I'd been earlier…" He shrugged.

"When I called the cops and they came something like two hours later, I was so mad at them I saw red. Jesus, you know they looked at him as if he was a piece of cold meat. One of them placed his fingers against Mike's neck above where the rope was fastened. He did that to check for a pulse.

"'Deader than a mackerel,' he said. 'His skin is cold. Probably's been hanging since last night.'

"That was his verdict. No expression of regret for another human being who lost the way. No regret, no sympathy, no kind word. Bastards! They didn't care."

John fell quiet, then he lifted his hand and shaded his eyes as he looked up into the brassy sky. Without changing his upward gaze, he said in a voice I had to strain to hear, "You know, a man doesn't need to reach for heaven. Heaven is always ready to stoop down to him."

He bowed his head and walked away with his shoulders hunched. I didn't see him again until the next day. By then he had recovered from his deep sadness but he was still moody.

I'm not sure what I expected to find in Mike's vandalized house. When later I interviewed the detective sergeant who had been in charge of the squad that searched my brother's house, he didn't bother to defend the destructive police methods.

"You can always file a claim," he said with a smirk, "not that it'll do much good. You being a visitor here, an outsider."

When I first saw the disarray in Mike's house, it appeared as if a wrecking crew had stormed through the first and second floors. Not a table, lamp or chair had been saved. The padded backs of chairs had been eviscerated. Stuffing and packing littered the floor where it had been thrown and trampled. Books were ripped, spines torn away; every cabinet and shelf where dishes and bric-a-brac had been displayed were swept clean, the broken refuse ground into the carpets under careless heels.

The medicine cabinet in the downstairs bathroom had

been emptied. Toothbrushes, dental paste, band aids, eye
drops, hair coloring, shampoo, a razor, a tube of athletes
foot cure, an empty bottle of Advil, dental floss and cotton
swabs, were heaped in the sink, splotched and dyed a garish
orange red from a bottle of Mercurochrome that had been
dropped on the hard porcelain surface. It had burst and
sprayed its contents, making a permanent stain. The top had
been removed from the toilet tank, and until I adjusted the
flush mechanism, the water in the toilet bowl swirled with a
protesting screech.

I couldn't adjust myself to the evidence of violence. I
knew nothing about police searches except from what I had
seen on television or in movies, but there was no question in
my mind that Mike's house had been ransacked, ruthlessly
destroyed. Nothing of value remained intact.

In the kitchen I found the drawers of silverware and
cooking utensils strewn on the floor. Knives, spoons, forks,
spatulas, sponges, dishwasher powder, a toaster and a
broken waffle iron were piled together in a forlorn heap on
the floor. Even the paper liners in the drawers had been torn
out and discarded on the linoleum tile that covered the
floor.

The refrigerator door gaped open, exposing the
shelves of perishable foods, as well as the freezer section, to
warm air. Thawed cartons of instant vegetables, orange
juice, milk, dripped and ran, leaving puddles on the floor
and attracting flies, ants and mosquitoes.

The longer I tramped through the ruined house, the
madder I got. I did preserve enough of a firm grasp on my
temper to acknowledge that there had to be a compelling
reason for cops, even for ones as irresponsible as the low-
grade goons who represented the Chilton police force, to
exert the determination and energy necessary to relentlessly

disembowel the house and its contents. Why?

More than fury that arises from bitter frustration and can be transformed into mindless rage, the devastation of the cops, I was certain cops been driven by an over-whelming urge to find something valuable Mike owned or possessed, or they thought he did. I'd learned from rumors I'd heard from the mourners at the showing of Mike's body at the funeral chapel, that he was supposed to have kept a secret ledger of sorts. Nobody could venture a guess what for. I had put the information aside as unimportant until I saw Mike's house. Then, I remembered a statement John Webb had made to me at the chapel. I had given little weight to it at the time, but now I could see that it may have been close to the truth. He had said he believed the cops were dirty, somehow indirectly involved in Mike's death through their connection with the person or persons who had killed Mike and arranged his body to look as if he had hanged himself.

As I righted an overturned kitchen chair and sat down for a minute, I thought more about John's idea of police involvement in the murder. It would account for their vindictive swath through the house. Had Mike kept a ledger? Why? If he had, what could he have written in it? As I thought back on the brother I knew, warm, open, cheerful, never secretive or conniving, I concluded that the whole idea of a journal or ledger was completely out of character for Mike.

Yet, it seemed to make absolute sense that something he knew or had done had resulted in his murder. Of that, without a shred of evidence to support my belief, I was absolutely certain. And just as certain was I that the cops had adopted the verdict of suicide in Mike's death as a camouflage for what they were covering up. I was going to make sure their nasty little scheme would be exposed.

It was at that moment I decided to reverse my earlier decision not to stay in the house. I certainly wasn't comfortable with the idea, but I knew I had to have an inexpensive base of operations from which to launch my investigation. My father's home in Gunbarrel was too far away, and since privacy was essential I couldn't ask my brother, Stewart, who was three years older than Mike, to allow me to stay with him.

Stewart, who also worked for WalMart in Chilton, was an ex-marine and lived in Chilton about four miles across town. I didn't want to involve Stewart and if I stayed with him what I intended to do inevitably would come out. A nice guy, Stewart didn't like surprises; he had built an orderly life, enjoyed predictability in his routine and found disturbing events dismaying. His focused approach had served him well in the Marine Corps and in the warehouse shipping job he filled at WalMart.

If I was going to stay in Mike's ravaged house, I had to clean the kitchen and make order in the bedroom where Mike had slept, and where I would replace him. The first order of business was for me to remove the broken dishes, silverware and cutlery from the dirty kitchen floor. I separated the broken pieces from the salvageable items and threw the discards into a plastic garbage can in which I placed a dark khaki bag as a receptacle.

After washing and drying the saved dishes and utensils, I attacked the refrigerator, discarding spoiled food and vegetables. By the time I had emptied the fridge, and washed, sponged and dried the white interior walls, I began to have hope of a new beginning.

It was several hours, however, before I had stored

pans, utensils, towels, and drawer liners where they belonged, washed the floor on my hands and knees and viewed my handiwork with approval. Before ascending the stairs to restore order to Mike's ravaged bathroom and bedroom, I made a list, sitting at the table, of supplies I would need to restock the kitchen and fridge.

I had no idea where Matt was or when he would return. At that moment, I did not care. One glance in his room — the picture of a solitary cell occupied by a sleeper who had surrendered his self respect — was enough to convince me that while the cops had tossed his sanctuary as thoroughly as the rest of the house, his own slovenliness had preceded the official visit. Though I had no experience with junkies, I was convinced Matt had abandoned his pride and identity to the deadly white powder he stuffed up his nose. I didn't know how he could afford his habit, and the line of speculation that opened in my mind leading to the betrayal of his father to pay for the monkey on his back made me sick. I knew Matt had fallen as close to the bottom as he could get. When the day of reckoning came, he was going to have to pay a terrible price that might mean the forfeit of his life in settlement.

It was about nine o' clock that night when Matt came stumbling home, unsteadily propped his bicycle against the railing on the front porch, and plodded up the stairs to his room. I intercepted him on the landing and he stepped back with a look of surprise and guilt on his face.

"I …uh, hello, Aunt Pam," he stammered. "What are you doing here?"

I didn't answer him immediately. Even from three feet away in the light of the hallway, I could see how big the pupils of his eyes were. Drugs like cocaine enlarge the pupils. I debated briefly whether to confront Matt now while he was still high, or wait until he had slept away his buzz. I decided he would probably be more talkative now than when he woke up. Depending on how much of a habit he was carrying, the interval of sleep might end with a sharp craving which would have to be served before he could function.

"Let's sit down and talk, Matt," I said. "We can go into your father's room. I'm sleeping there now until I return to Oregon."

I turned and walked the few steps that took me to Mike's room. I heard Matt follow, reluctantly, I was certain. I sat on the bed and pointed for Matt to take the chair in the corner by the lamp.

Matt hesitated at the door as he surveyed the room, then said awkwardly, "You've cleaned it up."

"Yes," I replied, "and you should do the same for your own room."

He sat down, plainly uncomfortable with a confrontation with his aunt, indicating his eagerness to go by his narrow perch on the edge of the chair.

"This won't take long," I assured him and watched him visibly relax. "I really have only one question, Matt. About what time was it when you heard your father's killers thumping around downstairs? Did you go downstairs when you heard them leave, or stay in bed?"

My question was double-barreled and I expected a sharp reaction from Matt. I wasn't disappointed. His eyes widened and his complexion blanched. "I — I don't know what you're talking about..."

"Oh, yes you do, Matt. One of the troubles with cocaine or any drug is that it loosens the tongue. Just like it did the day you found your dad in the backyard and you told Mrs. Webb next door that you heard noises about midnight.

It was the ladder from the garage where Mike kept it, falling against the side of the house. Now, he didn't remove it, did he? No, somebody else did. One of the people who killed him, maybe. What do you think?"

"I don't know," he cried. Suddenly, his face crumpled, grew shiny, wrinkled and red and ran with tears.

"I don't know," he blurted. "I was scared. I didn't know who was down there. Someone. I thought maybe they were trying to get in the house and I didn't know what to do. Dad wasn't home. In the last couple of months, he was gone lots of times. And he came home late. I missed him."

Matt took in deep gulps of air as if he were swallowing water to drown a deep thirst, and fresh tears popped out of his eyes. "What am I going to do? I'm just a dumb kid. Who's gonna take care of me?"

He buried his head in his arms propped on the side of the chair, with his shoulders heaving, and wept as if his heart would break.

I got up then and tenderly placed my hand on the back of his head. "We'll take care of you, son. We're not going to let you down. Don't you worry. Go on to bed now and have a good cry. It's time you did that. It's okay."

I was a little ashamed of myself for the way I had manipulated Matt, but I had to find out as much as he knew, which was nothing. He was a deeply frightened and confused boy who'd been deserted by the two parents in his life: his mother when she left his father, his father when he became so embroiled with his own disappointments and frustrations that he left his son to drift, to become an easy victim of the people with the dream powders, the terrible sweet and fascinating poisons that gradually subdue the will and kill the mind.

Unanswered for me as I helped my dear, blubbering

nephew to bed, was the major question, where did he get the money to pay for the drugs?

The next morning before Matt woke up I called my father in Gunbarrel. If I drove Matt to him would he take in his grandson? My father's answer was a small roar in my ear.

"What's got into you, Sis? You know better than to insult me with a question like that. Get him over here. I'll take care of him."

Following my trip to Gunbarrel, I called on Sergeant Pete Maddox, who had a desk in a large room where other detectives hung out off the main hallway of the Police and Justice Building across the street from the county court-house in the center square of Chilton. Big shady oak trees dappled the green lawns with deep shadows.

I didn't expect much from Maddox and he didn't surprise me with courtesy, civility or an open mind. He was a chain smoker, a lighted cigarette dangling from his lower lip and leaking smoke into his left eye. When he motioned me into the yellow walnut chair that sat beside his desk, I noticed his first two fingers on his right hand were stained a deep ochre color. I wondered what his lungs looked like. He fixed me with insolent, pouchy bloodshot eyes and said, "I've got other things to do, Ma'am, I know why you're here and we're going to keep this short. Your brother committed suicide. We confirmed our own findings with a formal autopsy in the Dallas County Medical Examiner's Office. That cost the city a pretty good piece of change. We could have used it more wisely for other more important things.

"We've heard from members of your family, including your father, who did not like the way we investigated your brother's death.

"I'm not going to apologize or waste my breath justifying our methods. If you have any complaints take them up with the city attorney. On your way out, stop at the sergeant's desk in the lobby. He has a paper sack with money and papers that belong to you. That's all, Ma'am."

He got up from his swivel chair and walked to the water cooler, his back turned indifferently in my direction.

My whole visit to the Chilton Police Department lasted five minutes. The only words he had permitted me to utter were my name and my relationship to Mike Penrose.

On my way out of the police station, I stopped at the sergeant's desk near the main entrance. Without a word, he handed me a form to sign, examined my signature, then thrust a paper sack at me. In the van a few minutes later, I discovered it contained Mike's wallet. There was a picture of me in it with Mike at my side. We were standing near the edge of a blue stream with fir trees in the background. I knew instantly when the photo had been taken. From my camera with a delayed action feature, that allowed Mike and I the time to prepare ourselves for the shot. The photo was seven years old. We'd gone fishing together and had gotten skunked.

There were car keys, a bank deposit receipt, a prescription with Mike's name on it for Valium from a local physician, a small pocket knife, forty-five dollars in currency, and a folded napkin from a bar with the name Mary and a phone number scribbled on it. Not much of a reminder of an ordinary man who lived thirty-six years and ended his life with a piece of hemp around his neck.

As I drove to Mike's house with a heavy sense of defeat riding on my shoulders, I thought about sergeant Maddox for just a moment. I realized he regarded me and my family with so little concern for any waves we could make, that he treated me with little more than contempt.

My cheeks burned as I recalled how quickly he had brushed me off, walking away to the water fountain as if I had never existed.

It was humiliating, but if I allowed myself to dwell on the rebuke, I'd never get anywhere with Mike's murder. Then, like a lark bringing a sweet note to charm the grey out of a flat morning, I remembered a cheerful, nonsensical ditty by an obscure poet whose name and rhyme I memorized when I was in the fourth grade in Artesia, California. On Fridays, our teacher, Miss Phelps, encouraged us to recite poems we had selected. When my turn came I stood up and said, "A poem by Charles Edward Carryl, entitled Robinson Crusoe:

> *The night was thick and hazy*
> *when the Piccadilly Daisy*
> *carried down the crew and captain in the sea;*
> *and I think the water drowned 'em,*
> *for they never ever found 'em,*
> *and I know they didn't come ashore with me.*

My sense of humor was restored by that little fragment; I was glad I remembered it. People need tiny inspirations, I acknowledged, particularly when the course they are following is winding, treachcrous and dangerous.

I sat in the van in front of Mike's house for fifteen minutes or so before I could reach a decision about my next step. I reviewed what I had learned, which was strong on suspicions and suppositions but weak on facts for proof of Mike's murder.

I rubbed my hand in the thick fur behind Red's ears,

thankful for my four-legged Labrador friend who never complained when I left him for long periods in the van, of course with water and a bone to chew on.

He put his head in my lap and raised his eyes at me as if to ask, What's our next move, pal?

"I don't know, Red," I said. "I think I've got to start asking questions. Mike was drinking a lot. The bars and taverns he visited might have heard things, picked up conversations, comments, opinions that might give me a lead. I think I'll try that. Ask questions, leave my business card every place I stop. Maybe we'll hit paydirt." That was the moment I remembered the folded bar napkin with the phone number and name.

I realized as I looked at my watch that it was seven o'clock, too late for me to start making enquiries about Mike at bars and taverns. Sure, they'd be open for business, but I wanted to make my calls about four in the afternoon before the regulars drifted in, before the bartenders got too busy to concentrate on my questions about Mike. I decided to warm up a T.V. dinner, and watch the boob tube in Mike's bedroom until I fell asleep.

As I donned my cotton nightshirt and tucked myself into Mike's spacious bed I almost regretted driving Matt to my dad's in Gunbarrel. I wasn't even sure the boy would stay more than the few days it would it take him to get straightened out a little bit.

Right then, I would have welcomed Matt back with open arms. At least he would be another warm body in the house where I heard noises I could not identify, whisper-ings, slight rustlings and vague thumps that set my heart racing. For the life of me I could not fathom how Matt could have stayed in his father's house a whole week after Mike had died. Also I had to admit that my brothers and sisters had failed in their responsibility to take him in. Unless, of course, he had elected to stay alone.

Red curled up on the floor next to the side of the bed I occupied and I must have fallen asleep with the T.V. on. But it was Red who woke me up with a deep growling in his throat about four a.m.

When my sleep-fogged brain grasped the meaning of Red's guttural growling, the voice he used when he was apprehensive or on guard against an unknown threat, my eyes flew open. I threw the covers off of me, switched on the bedstand lamp, and reached under my pillow for the stun gun I carried with me always.

With my left hand, I ran my fingers under the raised fur on the back of Red's neck. With a swift swiveling motion, he turned his head, looked me in the eyes to confirm his state of arousal, then rigidly faced the closed bedroom door and barked furiously. I was encouraged by his excited, threatening voice. Holding the stun gun firmly in my right hand, I moved quickly to the left side of the bedroom door where the knob was. With a quick motion, I threw the door open so that it swung away to my right and banged against the wall.

Light from the bedstand lamp flooded the dark hallway, revealing the absence of any threatening figure. I grabbed the powerful flashlight I had earlier placed in the bedstand drawer, and with Red at my side, now silent, walked down the hallway, snapping on electric lights as I came to them.

In this fashion, Red and I explored the house, room by room, but found absolutely nothing to alert him or me. Finally, knowing I would not sleep again that night, I walked to the kitchen made coffee and toast, and peeled an orange. Red was pleased with the remainder of a T.V. dinner

I warmed for him in the microwave. I was never more than a step away during my breakfast preparations from my stun gun which I laid on the tiled counter next to the sink.

Though I had used the stun gun twice since I had bought it and started carrying it in my roomy purse, on both occasions, the men who insisted on bothering me were less than three feet away and groping me with their hands when I pressed the barrel against their chests and pulled the trigger. The electric charge hit them like a heavy fist and drove them to their knees.

Of course, distance was the limiting factor for my defensive weapon. Unless I could apply it directly to an attacker's body, it was useless. I never deluded myself about the range and effectiveness of the gun, but I admit holding it — an impressive black pistol that resembled an automatic — gave me comfort and reassurance. Most people, I realized, would not know the difference between it and a weapon that shot bullets instead of electric impulses.

Two hours later, with the sun up and the temperature growing hot outside, I fell asleep on the living room couch, Red laying nearby on the littered carpet, still uncleaned from the police visit.

It was noon when I revived, then spent the next four hours with trash bags and a vacuum cleaner restoring the downstairs.

My opinion of the Chilton cops sank even lower when I discovered among the siftings destined for the trash collector what appeared to be a wrinkled page torn from a daily appointment book. Rule lines segmented each week into calender days. As I examined the scribbled writing that continued across the lines, I recognized Mike's hard-to-read letters jammed tightly together. My excitement took a leap at what I was able to decipher after I found a blank pad and

pen in my purse and translated the scrawled words onto a
clean page. What I read was both puzzling and mysterious.
According to my interpretation, on June 25, just about two
months earlier, Mike had made this note to himself:

"One wooden crate in the deliveries tonight was a lot
heavier than the others, and it smelled to high heaven. I
knew better than to open it. It was stapled tightly and it
would be hard for me to duplicate how it was closed even if
I was stupid enough to pry it open.

"One thing for sure, though, whatever is in there is
dead now, and it's deteriorating, I don't even want to think
what it might be part of. It sure smells terrible. What makes
me worried is that they'd put something like this in my
deliveries. Is this a test that I can keep my mouth shut, or
what?"

I carefully smoothed and folded the torn page and
placed it in a small pocket in my purse that held a tiny
mirror. It disappeared snugly behind the mirror. I had never
been superstitious, but the paper seemed to me like a direct
communication from Mike beyond the grave. It had to be
something like that, or maybe it was a message from God.
That was quite a notion! But I remembered strange
comforting visitations from a figure I decided was an angel
when I was a lot younger.

I'd never prayed to God much and I knew Mike was
more spiritually oriented than I. Anyway, I thought it was
remarkable that the wrinkled page had survived the drastic
search mounted by the Chilton cops. That idea drew me to
another crucial consideration. What if the police had
discovered the whole calender book filled with writings
from Mike? Was this the rumored ledger folks at Mike's
funeral had gossiped about? The page I'd found was from a
small book, one that would easily fit into a man's pants

pocket with hardly a bulge. My intuition told me that Mike, who liked to make notes to remind himself of things to do, would have found a small calender book convenient to carry and put down his thoughts in temporary form until he could elaborate on them later more fully in a larger journal.

I liked that idea. It appealed to my familiarity with the way my brother's brain worked. It fit, and that meant it was probable that the cops had found the small portable book Mike had traveled with. Where in the house they had located it, I had no idea.

If that supposition were true, it was another fact for me to place in my own mental record of duplicitous actions by the Chilton police. They weren't giving up any secrets they had gathered and they were sequestering knowledge about events and evidence related to Mike's murder which they insisted officially, as recently as yesterday, was suicide.

When I visited the insolent and insulting Sergeant Maddox, he had confirmed the suicide verdict as coldly and without consideration for my feelings as he could manage. There were not many people I learned to dislike or hate in an instant, but Maddox's behavior was indefensible and his rude contemptuous manner deserved nothing better than intense scorn.

Now, I realized it was time for me to start tavern and bar hopping in search of information on people who knew Mike and might have valuable tips about the lowlifes with whom he was associated. Based on what he had written on the torn page I'd found, there seemed to be little doubt that his off-hours employers were unconscionable, unsavory and on the bent side of the law. Most probably they were the killers who had ended his life.

The cocktail napkin that had been part of Mike's effects turned over to me at the police station guided me to a barn-like red tavern occupying about half a block on a street named Highpoint. The big sign atop the long, slanting roof bore the name: Harry's Texas Bar.

It was three-thirty on a blistering Texas afternoon, too hot to leave Red in the van. There was deep shade under a long roof overhang and there he found himself a place to curl up.

In the pleasant artificial gloom of the interior, cool with icy blasts from overhead air conditioners, two bartenders stood at opposite ends of a mahogany bar which I estimated to be at least one hundred and fifty feet long.

I seated myself on a stool close to the nearest bartender and ordered a glass of sparkling water with lime and ice. When he returned with my drink, I asked him if he had known Mike Penrose.

He was a big man with receding brown hair, a long puffy nose, and thick broad lips. A huge chest expanse covered with a sparkling white shirt was adorned with onyx cuff links at the sleeves and a red bow tie at the collar. Pinned on his shirt pocket was a shiny badge announcing Harry's Texas Bar. Below the title was the bartender's name, George Foster, printed in bright red letters.

"You're not from Texas. I can tell that," George said affably. "Down here we're careful about the questions we ask. I haven't seen Mike for a few days. The best thing for you to do is hang around here after about nine tonight. He generally shows up here three, four times a week. That's the best I can do for you. No offense."

"No offense taken," I said. "I'm his sister from Oregon. I came down for his funeral. It was the day before yesterday."

George frowned and leaned toward me with his massive elbows on the bar supporting his weight.

"What happened to him?" he asked.

"Well, the police say it was suicide, but I don't believe it, no more than his friends and the rest of his family."

"Doesn't seem likely to me either," George said. "How can I help you?"

"Well," I said, "I came across the name Mary in some of his personal effects. I thought I'd try to find her. I got the impression that he knew her pretty well. Maybe — she can tell me what was going on in his life."

George straightened; he seemed to withdraw from his cooperative attitude and said with a remote tone of voice, "I know her. She comes in here…"

He hesitated for an awkward moment, then leaned forward again.

"Ma'am," he said, "you seem like a nice person. If I were you, I wouldn't get involved with Mary. You have to decide. If you insist, you can write your name and phone number and I'll give it to her when she comes in."

I removed a business card with my Oregon phone number. I penciled in my local phone number at Mike's deserted house on the slim chance that Mary might call me from Harry's Texas Bar before I left the state.

I gave the card to George with a five dollar bill. He looked at the bank note gravely, then said, "That's not necessary, Ma'am."

"I know," I said, "but it would please me if you'd take it." I added, "Mike was murdered. I know it and so do a lot of others. I've got to get to the bottom of it. If that means meeting some strange people, I'm ready for that. I'll be available until tomorrow morning but I will accept long distance calls if anybody wants to reach me in Portland."

George looked directly into my eyes for a moment, then made a small smile with his lips. "Yes, ma'am. I

believe you are ready. I'll leave your card for Mary. She'll
be in, you can count on it."

It was six o'clock when I exited the seventh and final
bar I canvassed to ask about Mike. In two I encountered
strong hostility and grim faces with straight-lined mouths;
people obdurately refused to answer any questions and
made it plain I was unwelcome. In two other bars, Mike was
unknown. Three were acquainted with his name and
promised to hand out my cards to any of the regulars who
may have known Mike well.

I decided I would not stay in Mike's house another
night. Instead, I'd drive to Gunbarrel, bunk with Dad and
leave for Oregon early in the morning. I did stop at Mike's
whispering two-story long enough to take the few things I
had left behind in his bedroom.

I drove from Chilton directly to Gunbarrel, stopping
only long enough to buy a Texas barbequed beef sandwich
and coffee, both to go at one of those incomparable, shabby
roadside stands where beef, pork and cabrito are slow-
roasted and sliced for the meal of your life. No other state
I've traveled in has mastered the art of Texas barbeque.

I greeted my dad when I arrived, then surprised myself
by asking to use his phone to call Mike's phone for any
messages. It was foolish, but I dialed the code number for
messages and to my astonishment, there was voicemail
from Mary.

She said if I were to show up at Harry's Texas Bar
between eleven and eleven-thirty that same night we could
talk about Mike. She said she had plenty to say. And she
assured me that this was true. She warned me, however, that
she would not wait after eleven-thirty.

It was eight o'clock when I left Gunbarrel. I figured
I'd make the ninety mile run in about an hour and fifteen

minutes with a good margin of time to spare. I almost made it, but four miles from Chilton on the outskirts I heard a sharp pop and a noisy, rattling bumping and my van rolled to a stop. I found the trouble as soon as I lifted the hood. My heart sank as I saw the ruined fan belt. It was three hours after I caught a ride to a busy service station and the owner finally agreed to drive me back to my parked van and install a new belt.

Of course, when I called Harry's Texas Bar about twelve-thirty or so, I learned Mary had left long ago.

Chapter Four

It was wrong of me to think that I had accomplished very little in Texas except to say goodbye to my kid brother. But I carried my dissatisfaction with myself for failing to connect with Mary, like an irritating grudge, until I was about eighty miles west of Gunbarrel on the road to Oregon. Finally, I quit cursing the fate that had snapped the tired fan belt in my van, and made peace with myself by constructing a mental list of my achievements in Chilton. As I reviewed my activities in the Southwest Texas town which I believed ran with a deep undercurrent of criminal conspiracy, I felt much better about what I had learned and realized I had been lucky, not wise, to escape injury or worse.

When it came down to it, I had challenged a Superior Court Judge, conspired with John Webb to subvert evidence (his photos of Mike in his death pose) and concealed what could turn out to be vital evidence (the torn page from the small daily calender) for the motive behind Mike's murder.

The fact was that I had done a lot during my three days in Texas, the most singular achievement of which was proving to myself beyond any shred of doubt that Mike's death was a brutal homicide. I still did not know who had done it, but I had stumbled onto a woman who admitted frankly in a phone message that she knew a lot about Mike, and presumably, could tell me about what led to his death.

Bad luck may have postponed our meeting, but a reliable voice inside me assured me that we would arrange a new rendezvous.

I felt better about myself after giving myself credit for what I had done, and I let the rolling miles beneath the wheels of my van make a sort of moving tattoo that was like a pleasant and repetitive musical theme. It was accompanied by cloudbursts that drummed the steaming asphalt with watery spikes and soaked the air with mugginess and moisture.

When I said goodbye to my father and saw again the pain that had not left his eyes, my heart went out to him. Gruff old man with a history of violence and alcohol madness, still his heart was sterling and I knew it was heavy with his son's death. I had lost a brother, but he had lost a son. I gave him a bear hug, one also to my nephew, Matt, and headed down the road.

My old van took me west like an enthusiastic teenager rushing to the mall, and I settled deeper into my seat behind the wheel. I rolled up the window when the pouring rain beat against the windshield with such ferocity that my vision was blurred and I took my foot off the accelerator. After the storm passed, I turned the air conditioner on high to banish the cloying humidity.

I glanced briefly into the mirror on the visor and was surprised at who stared back at me. God, I looked like hell.

My moist hair clung to my scalp in stringy strands. My skin was a dull shade of muddy grey, and was covered with a film of fine moisture. I looked and felt as if I hadn't slept for weeks. Well, the nights in Mike's house had terrified me.

Sleep was probably more important to me than to other people because mine had been interrupted so often by monster dreams from the time I was about seven years old. I lived then in Artesia, California, and I dreaded going to bed because of what was in store for me so often. I clearly recalled those terrible nights when I would snuggle deep into the warm folds of my blankets, praying I would not have one of my terrifying dreams. They always woke me with a thundering heart and a clutching fear that I was about to die. Whenever I was assaulted by such a nightmare, I'd throw the covers aside and bolt out of bed to the closet in my room, hiding behind my clothes that hung from the pole suspended between the walls. There I stayed in a dark corner haunted by frightening visions and shivering with terror, until I worked up enough courage to run into the living room and switch on the television set. I kept the volume low and watched the comforting images on the screen until I fell into an exhausted sleep on the couch or until the morning light chased away the shadows.

Now, I was penetrating deeper into the West Texas countryside, empty of signs of life, it seemed, except for the turkey buzzards that tirelessly roamed the blue skies with telescopic eyes for dead and dying animals far below.

Reluctantly, my mind returned to the past and I remembered a particular night when I had fallen into a deep sleep, but strangely saw an image of myself as an infant secure in a bassinet perched in the back seat of my father's car. Usually, when a terrifying dream was about to take shape in my consciousness, I would be warned

with a sinking feeling that it was going to be bad. But on
this occasion in my dream mind, the picture of myself —
a dark-haired little two-year-old girl with rosy cheeks,
just a baby — assured me that there was nothing to worry
about.

I saw my father behind the wheel, steering erratically,
and pounding my mother with his brutal voice which drew
her silent tears. Strangely enough I, the baby, was not
screaming with fright from my father's awful shouting
anger and his maniacal driving. Suddenly, he whipped the
steering wheel in a sharp turn that drew screeching protests
from the tires as the car lurched violently to the right. At
that moment the rear door flew open and I was wrenched
from the bassinet and hurled out into the traffic. My mother
turned in her seat as I flew from my safe perch through the
open space of the outflung door. I saw my little body make
an arc, and with a thump, I landed on the hood of a truck
trailing behind our car. Then I fell beneath the speeding
truck. As I slipped to the ground, I heard my mother
screaming at my father to strop the car.

It was at that same heart-stopping moment in my
dream that I witnessed a smokey-blue cloud appear,
approach me, hover, and vanish like a sudden wind. As the
cloud passed, a marvelous feeling of well-being swept over
me and imparted the knowledge that I, the baby, was safe,
enfolded protectively in the arms of an angel. My baby-self
was alive and safe. I did not die under the wheels of the
pickup truck, and I knew this as a solemn, incontrovertible
truth that nothing could change. That baby, that tiny me, had
been saved by an angel.

I vividly remembered what happened at the breakfast
table the next morning. While I was eating my oatmeal, my
mother, lingering over her coffee, seemed strangely quiet,

perturbed, her brow wrinkled as if she were searching for the right words to convey a special thought.

Finally, she said, "I think you're old enough for me to tell you about something that happened to you when you were just a baby."

I looked at Mom, wondering what kind of a story she would tell me. I loved stories. It was obvious that she had chosen her words carefully when she said, "When you were little, oh, about four months, you were in the car with your dad and me when he took a sharp turn. The rear door whipped open and you flew out of your bassinet. I guess the door hadn't been closed properly.

"Anyway, you bounced off a pickup in the next lane and ended up beneath the wheels. It all happened so fast that there was nothing I could do. I thought I'd go crazy, out of my mind. Well, the pickup passed over you. Your face was a little bit scraped, but miraculously, you were not injured. The police arrived on the scene and called an ambulance. You were examined at the hospital and everybody there said it was a miracle you were alive. I thank God for saving you. Whenever you get sick or overtired, you can still see the little scars on your face. They show up then!"

My mother looked at me expectantly, but I sat still holding my tongue. I was incredulous that somehow she knew about my dream. My secret! I had not whispered a word about it. I never told my parents or anybody about my dreams. Even when they were horrible and frightening, I kept them to myself. How could she know? Confused, I got up from the table and ran to my room trying to figure out how she could have penetrated my mind. I was sitting on the edge of my bed, miserable and confused, when I felt a strange warmth and a sense of love settle over me. In all of my short life nothing in my brief experience prepared me for the rapture, for the expansion of my heart, the lifting of my spirit — my whole body seemed to open like the petals of a flower greeting the sun. Although I had no words of explanation for the deep understanding that flowed into my mind, I knew in my child's heart that the source of power came from the same angelic visitor who had clasped my infant body when I flew out of the car all those years earlier and saved my life.

My reminiscing had slowed my driving speed, and I was about to accelerate when I noticed the blinking sign of a roadside café beckoning. I could see the place had once been a Mexican sod house, now enlarged, painted a drab pink. I made a bet with myself that the thick walls stood off the heat that collected in the mesquite and sagebrush and in the low-growing dusty creosote bushes the Mexicans called hedionotilla, or "the little stinkers."

It was still raining when I parked in front of the café-tavern-one pump gas station that sat in solitary isolation with no visible signs of people nearby. A stale beer-flavored atmosphere thick with smoke-layered air greeted me as I made my way to a table inside. It was only nine o'clock in the morning, but two sturdy West Texans hugged the bar, nursing their breakfast beer and watching the morning news, probably from Abilene, on a small television set on the counter.

The dark Mexican woman behind the bar left her place, picked up a steaming pot, stopped at my table, greeted me with "Buenos dias," and poured a hot cup of coffee for me.

"No thanks," I said to her offer of food. "I don't want anything to eat. Just the coffee, please."

The place was oppressive in a colorless and used-up way. Neon signs blinked names of popular beers, tired posters with curled-up edges advertising Coke and chili hung from the walls, along with a collection of old license plates and a clutch of yellowing bumper stickers with their fading messages. I asked for a big container of coffee to go, paid my tab, left a suitable tip, and headed back on the road. I was resigned to the countless miles I had to go with only myself for company. It was quite all right. Even though my brother's death was still uppermost in my mind, I had accepted Mike's own culpability for his murder. My mind took me back to the few times we had talked about what we would do with our lives. I recalled one time when I had just completed two years of college and had offered Mike some of the exciting ideas I had learned from reading about the great thinkers who had left indelible prints on the record of human history.

I had approved of my kid brother's strong interest in auto mechanics. It was only natural, his being the son of a man who was a genius, who at one time in his remarkable career had operated one of the largest lawnmower repair services in Southern California.

While I applauded Mike's genius for diagnosing and repairing trouble in engines, I tried to stir in him an intellectual interest that would take him further than dirty fingernails and buddies whose pastime was beer, pool and women looking for a meal ticket. I tried to make him understand that every person ought to be inquisitive through every day of his life, that it should be a compelling adventure up until the moment when he no longer cast a shadow in the sun.

I chewed on my lip as I realized that Mike had gone off the track. He'd become his own worst mistake. I loved him, I would do my darnedest to find his killers, but I wasn't blind to his failures. I was certain he had died without making in his life one outstanding significance. Some accomplishment that gave him a strong excuse for having been born, for taking up space.

I wiped the tears from my eyes, but I still grieved inside for the promise of himself that Mike failed to embrace.

Of course, I was not without guilt for making excuses myself.

My reflections on Mike's lack of passion led me to admit that I needed to examine my own life, dig deeply for some answers. "They" say we carry with us the events that have made lasting impressions on our consciousness, which in turn dictate the direction in which we travel. In other words, we all have ghosts from the nursery.

Boy, did I have ghosts.

I loved my mother and father and I respected them, in spite of the fact that my childhood years were spent in fear, in the unhealthy atmosphere of physical abuse. I remember my tall father beating the holy pudding out of my tiny mother when he was drinking. And on top of that, he beat my sister and my brothers. I was scared to death of him. I made sure to stay out of his way and try not to do anything that would tick him off. I was the only one he never laid a hand on. And I never fathomed why.

Drinking brought out the monster in him most times and the great charmer at others. Later, when I was in my teens, I felt uncomfortable about having my girlfriends around when Dad was in one of his "affectionate" moods. Alcohol can make such a fool out of people, and my father, with booze in him, had the morals of an alley cat.

I could still see the look on my mother's face — the hurt, the humiliation and the deadly resignation that settled over her features after one of the violent episodes my dad created. He churned the fires of dispute with the same dedication he devoted to drinking. Mom was scared to death of him; why she stayed with him all those years, I never knew. She had no self-confidence. She was a beautiful, smart woman but did not know it. In the end, my mother found the courage to break her husband of his abusive behavior. We all cheered her and thought if only she had acted sooner, she could have spared herself and us the physical and emotional changes that come to victims of repeated batterings.

The event that culminated in my mother's desperate act happened when Dad slapped her face while he was raging with alcohol. My mother reached for an oak dining room chair when his back was turned, and raising it as high as her arms could reach, she swung it down on his unsuspecting back. He fell to the floor like a poled ox and lay unconscious for half an hour. When he revived, shaken, his rage replaced with surprise, shame and regret, amazingly he turned a new leaf. It was too late for me, the oldest, to benefit from his new behavior. By then, I was twenty-one and had been supporting myself away from the house for three years, and battling my own phantoms.

But while I was growing up and still at home I hid under my bed in my room or burrowed into my closet with my eyes squinched shut, and put my hands over my ears to block out the harsh sounds of violence raging in another part of the house.

As if my parents' bloody rows were not bad enough, my nightmares haunted me and I curled up with my pillow and told myself simple made-up stories to keep awake at night. I was dying to go to sleep, yet pinched myself, bathed my face with cold water, did anything to avoid closing my eyes. More than anything, the nightmares robbed me of the giddy carelessness that belongs to children.

The horror show behind my closed eyes took place in different settings, with different casts of people, but always the vivid performances depicted murder, killings, blood and gore. The horrible deeds most always involved members of my family, and try as I might to scream in order to warn my loved ones of impending danger, my voice was always silent. Where did all the garbage in my head come from? Why couldn't I dream of flowers and fairies and birthday parties, and picnics and Christmas? Other children did. I knew they did, for they told me their dreams in school. I could never talk about mine.

Thank God there was one place I loved to go to lose myself, to forget about my nightmares and feel loved. That place was the barn situated on our one acre of land, and it became my sanctuary where I felt safe and the animals became my friends and companions. They brought me their trust, their laughter and joy. All my pain washed away during the hours I spent with my animals.

We had a cow, a goat, chickens, banties, rabbits, ducks and geese. There were never any strings attached to their affections for people, and I was surrounded by all that love when I was with them. I knew my parents loved me, but they were always involved in violence or repairing themselves from the emotional injuries it produced. Not much was left of them to share with their children. The animals were a blessing. Alive, warm and demanding nothing, they allowed me to pet them, hold them, feel their warm response and sense their protective loyalty. Whenever a spanking loomed on the horizon for me, I'd run out of the house and head for the barn because I knew the animals would defend me.

My favorite pet was a white domestic duck named Quacker. She was one of the first animals I ever owned. She demonstrated her affection one day when I had done something, I didn't know what, to set off my dad. He chased me into the barn and was just about to paddle my bottom when Quacker attacked him, snapping viciously at his ankles. In his surprise and anger, Dad kicked back so hard he broke Quacker's neck. I was furious with him for killing something that I loved so dearly. I was so mad I wouldn't talk to him for weeks. After that incident, it seemed that Dad curbed his temper around me, and occasionally we talked things over when I got into trouble. Just the same, I was devastated by Quacker's death. She had protected me and had been killed for her loyalty.

My brothers and sisters knew better than to fight with me in the barn; the animals would rush to my rescue. Once, my chicken attacked my sister Melissa, flying onto her head and pecking viciously at her scalp. I'll never forget her hysterical screams as she danced from one foot to the other, trying to shake the angry chicken. Melissa never set foot in the barn again and to this day hates chickens.

By the time I was fifteen, I had perfected my sleep walking techniques, and often wandered from the house in the middle of the night, driven out of bed by my terrifying nightmares. Locked doors wouldn't keep me in, bad weather didn't faze me, and the quiet streets of our neighborhood witnessed my pattering, naked feet in silence. Dressed only in my thin nightgown, I'd go as far as a neighbor's house and sit on a porch step with my arms wrapped around myself, still soundly asleep.

My mom told me that I strayed much further than the close neighbors on many nights. On one nocturnal roaming, I wandered more than three miles away from home before I was picked up by the police. Mother reported that the police got well-acquainted with me, and knew instantly who to call when someone reported a girl in a nightgown walking in her sleep. My trips took me far afield, I was discovered by cruising patrol cars who had been alerted to my habits, and they took me home. Mother told me there were many times when her maternal warning system woke her. She learned to check if I were in my bed. When she found me gone, she'd throw a coat over her nightgown and run out the door which I always left open in my haste to escape the night goblins who pursued me until I outdistanced them. Mom found me every time, carried me back to the house, then tucked me into bed. When I awoke in the morning, the ghost of the nightmare lingered as a heavy weight on my heart, yet never did I have a single recollection of wandering the streets in my sleep.

The rain stopped as I drove my van into the small West Texas town of Fort Stockton. I pulled off the road to get gas and to eat. I had driven a long stretch and I needed to move around and take the kinks out of my limbs. California was still a few hundred miles away.

I ate lunch at another roadhouse that was little different from the one before — just another Connie's-Café-and-Bar, smelling of stale booze and dead cigarettes, and with an undertone of garlic and overcooked coffee. I gazed out the window as I sipped my coffee and saw a young woman talking earnestly to a man about her own age. He had a sullen expression on his face and was slouching against a rain-washed blue pickup. Short, blondish hair decorated his scalp and reached out in all directions. Acne scars and pimples covered his face. Overly slim, his tight jeans clung to his bones like a paint job; certainly, he was no Robert Redford.

The more persuasively the girl spoke, the more the young man closed his face, sulked and turned away from her. Finally, he got into his truck which was parked in a small lake of water, and in spite of the girl's pleadings, slammed the door and roared away, splashing a stream of mud on her legs.

When she lifted her face, tears ran down her cheeks. She was desolated. I wondered what her life was like. She seemed so young to be so sad. I wanted to go outside and give her a big hug and some imperishable wisdom that would clear the storm from her face, but I had no such asset to pass on. I wanted to tell her to let her boyfriend go, that she was worth a better mate, and a better fate. Funny, but I was in the same boat, a little older than she but no wiser, and I didn't want to know it. I sat still, finishing my greasy hamburger, remembering when I was eighteen and had left home to be on my own.

After I graduated from high school, I left my parents' house. It was high time. As much as I loved my mother and father, I felt I had overstayed my welcome, mostly because of their problems. I no longer wanted to be in their presence, a party to their endless rows. When would they end? When would my mother do something for herself?

A friend of mine and I decided to share living quarters and we found a little house in Anaheim, California. The place had a good feeling of home and afforded us both some privacy, and we got along well. I took a full load at college, had a full-time job in a dress shop, and as if those activities weren't enough to fill my plate, I partied a lot, danced into the wee hours of the night, boogied till I dropped. I gave the saying "burning the candle at both ends" a new meaning. I flew from one thing to the next, never once catching my breath. I thought I was having a great time. This was fun! I was catching up on life. Sure! Never having dated at home, I went from no dating to over-dating.

But I was miserable. I was tired. I barely ever slept. I sat up in bed dozing, my head growing heavy, nodding off for a split second, only to jerk awake as I fought the encroaching sleep. I mustn't sleep. I would dream. I would stand in paralyzed horror as the screen unfolded with evil, vile and horrible images of murder and with rivers of blood that sent me screaming into despair. Dark, ugly shadows chased me. I was scared to death. I was exhausted. I had to stop dreaming.

I was twenty-one years old, a grown woman terrified of phantoms, miserably caught up in the whirlwind of my own traitorous imagination. My grandmother had told me many times that I was a special kind of person, but it didn't mean anything. I couldn't see beyond my nose. I was emotionally dead, and if I didn't get some sleep I knew I would surely collapse. I had to rest. I was out of control. There was only one thing left for me to do: I had not tried prayer.

As I drove my little white van into El Paso's windy desert outskirts, I thought back to the incredible day that changed my life. I was a woman desperate for rest, solace, and release from the dark shadows that threatened my sanity. One day I came home in the early afternoon, frantic with a plan to sleep in broad daylight. Perhaps the dark monster dreams would fail to materialize in the light of the sun. I felt strange and disoriented and I started to cry. I hadn't cried for years. I'd been able to hide my tears with the same secrecy with which I cloaked my nightmares. "Show no woe, tell no woe," that was the way I had managed my life since childhood. Now, hot tears rose to my eyes and spilled over as I sank to my knees to pray. I asked God for help. I pleaded and beseeched Him. I prayed and I prayed.

I stayed on my knees for a long time. I don't remember the words I used or if I said anything at all, but I know I experienced an outpouring of emotions and feelings that I had kept bottled up for a very long time. Finally, I rose to my feet, went into my bedroom, stretched out on my bed and closed my eyes. I had done all I knew how to do and I invited sleep to come.

Then, as if I had stepped into a pool with warm water encroaching and lapping on my bare skin, I felt a gentle heat rise at my left side. I opened my eyes and saw a huge, shapeless, blue-white light hovering near and suspended in space. As I watched in awe, frightened and excited, the image of a small woman floated out from the center of the light. I reached out to touch her hooded cloak, but the figure moved beyond my fingers. I slowly leaned back against the headboard of my bed and the silent figure approached me again and came close. Slowly, she raised her arms and her hands and gently touched my body. From her hands flowed a healing warmth that came into my body from my head to my toes. I did not understand what was happening, but I was spellbound, and afraid at the same time that the lady was just another illusion, no different, but gentler, than my other dreams. Then, just as swiftly as she had appeared, the blue lady moved back into the center of the glowing bluish cloud which was still suspended in my room three feet away from my bed. When the light swallowed her up, the glow of the cloud grew fainter and fainter until it was gone. It disappeared just as quickly as it had materialized. My body relaxed, I closed my eyes and fell into a long deep sleep.

As I left Phoenix, Arizona behind, headed for Los Angeles, I remember waking after the visit of the little lady at peace and no longer afraid of the dark. I was infused with energy and gratitude which I had never before experienced.

I slid off my bed, dropped to my knees and gave thanks. Except for the one disturbing dream about Mike's death many, many years later, I never had another nightmare. The monsters vanished along with the blue lady and the white light.

I slept in Wickenburg, Arizona that night and planned an early start in the morning. I'd pick up my kids in Anaheim and head home. I had not the slightest doubt that I would hear from the woman named Mary when I got home to Gresham, Oregon.

Chapter Five

When I parked my van in front of my sister's house in Anaheim, California, where my mom was visiting, my children swarmed out to greet me and I hugged them until they squealed. I visited with my mom for a little while, but I was in a hurry to get home. I had work to do. The kids and I had been gone altogether about ten days and when we pulled into our own driveway, which was wet from a late summer storm, there stood Tom backlighted in the frame of the open door with his arms folded menacingly across his chest. I could have won a million dollar bet that he had been waiting with a head of steam building on his warped belief that I was unfair to him, did not caress his ego with deserved compliments, or treat him like the lord of the manor he wished to be. I didn't love him, he had told me a thousand times.

I was certain that he was still sore and resentful about my going to my brother's funeral and considered my trip to

Texas a traitorous desertion. Before I took my bags into the bedroom, I knew he would attack, and the fight he'd been justifying to himself would begin. As the kids and I trooped into the house, he used the familiar, "God, you look ugly," gambit to start the violence that would inevitably escalate into screaming accusations, vicious lies and four-letter words, designed to demean and punish. I could almost predict, depending on the circumstances, which little drama he would employ to humiliate, deride and tear me down.

It was the same old story every time I came home from a trip selling welding supplies, which was the way I brought a very good commission check home every month. Tom loved the extra money but hated the idea that my professional expertise was beyond his control.

Tom switched his attack strategy from insulting me for letting myself go to a more convenient accusation. He screamed that a phone call I had to make when I walked into the house took precedence over feeding my kids. When I walked into the kitchen, the children were sullen and hostile. Finally, my oldest son, Adam, with a burning face and tears of anger brimming in his eyes, accused me of not loving him and his brother and sister. Just then, Tom swaggered into the kitchen and stopped about three inches away from me, and with his chin protruding aggressively yelled, "You goddam bitch! You selfish, self-centered bitch. What kind of mother are you? You won't even fix a few goddam sandwiches for your children! You have no time for me either. You are always driving all over the goddam country. The dog gets more attention from you than I do. You...you...bitch! You're never home, you're always gone and you don't give a goddamned about me — you whore."

Almost unbidden, my right arm flew from my side and I delivered a haymaker to Tom's cheek. He retaliated with a sharp blow to my stomach. He struck me several more times. He yelled vile names at me and everybody in the kitchen was screaming. What hurt me far more than his blows was the terrible language directed scathingly at me from my kids. I was shattered and furious. I'd had enough! I pushed Tom away from me with all my strength and ran from the room, his vicious voice following me like an anvil hammered by ringing obscenities. I was tired, tired of it all. But, I told myself, I loved him. How could I? I thought, why was I there? Did I confuse commitment with love? I was confused. I would have to figure it out — tomorrow. Not that night with my head hurting and my arms and chest smarting from where his fists had landed.

I had only been home for a day, my brother's death still fresh in my mind, when another tragedy struck. Jesse, Tom's seventeen-year-old son, had been killed in an automobile accident in Florida where he worked. He had been driving too fast, hit a soft shoulder, flipped the truck he was driving and died instantly in the twisted wreckage. Oh, dear God, what next? I had been close to Jesse. He was like my own son and now he was gone. Like Mike.

Tom kept a stiff upper lip during the days of mourning, and sat unmoving, dry-eyed through the memorial services, which were held in Portland. Jesse was cremated in Florida and his ashes flown to Oregon. I looked at the container that held what was left of the boy he had been. The boy who lived in my heart was still strong, alive and vital. In that condition would I keep him in my memory, not in an urn.

I was at home in my quiet house when the phone rang. It was Mary from Texas! We both started talking at the same time, I apologizing for having missed her and she reiterating that she had warned me to be on time.

"I told you not to be late. You've got to listen to me if you want some help. You've got to play by my rules," she scolded in her husky voice. "I'm going to tell you things I shouldn't, and I'm going to be very careful. I don't want to end up like Mike. The people he ran with are a tough bunch. They have a big organization. Their web stretches from Mexico all over the U.S. They play for high stakes, and they don't allow mistakes."

"I'm sorry, Mary," I said. "The fan belt on my van broke just short of town."

"Okay, Okay, forget it," she said curtly. "Let's get on with things. I'll tell you what you want to know right now," Mary said in a hushed voice I could barely hear, "It is true, your hunch was correct. Mike was murdered."

When I heard Mary say the words that confirmed my own deep conviction, my heart pounded in my chest, and I heard myself say, "Oh, God, I knew it all the time." I just broke down.

I took a couple of deep breaths and asked, "Mary, what happened to my brother? What did he do to deserve to be killed? What happened?"

"It's a long story, Pam, " Mary said thoughtfully. "Let me tell you what I know."

In her flat, husky voice, Mary confirmed what Mike had said to me when we talked on the phone. He had been vague about things that were troubling him and made a reference to an IRS problem. I didn't question him. I also knew that he and his wife were not getting along. They had one of those on-again off-again marriages. Sometimes after a fight, she moved out for a period. Other times, it was Mike's responsibility to leave and bunk with a friend. Mike was drinking heavily. What had started with a beer or two had become a bad habit. He and Dawn-Lee, his wife, fought often about money — they never had enough. Chilton was certainly not a boom town, and for a mechanic like Mike, business was slow. He didn't earn very much at his job with WalMart. His heavy drinking precipitated the fights with his wife. He admitted that he had beaten Dawn-Lee, and confessed that he was beside himself with guilt and remorse for what he had done to her.

"About six years ago, " Mary said, "Mike was really at loose ends, nothing was going right for him when all of a sudden, opportunity knocked, or, so he thought. Nothing was going right. That's when it all started. Mike got into trouble because he didn't realize how the guys I told you about worked. He really never bothered to find out who they were. All he saw was the bait they dangled — money, and he jumped at it.

"There was one night that Mike sat at the bar at Harry's and complained that he never had enough money to do anything. His wife was on his back all the time for not earning a decent living and he blamed himself for her unhappiness."

With strong irony, as if relating Mike's story to her own unhappy life, Mary said, "The people in the organization know just how to find the weak spots in a person. They look for the money hungry and the insecure, and recruit them into a game they later regret. By then, it's too late. They've got you by the balls and they own your life."

"Well," Mary said, pausing for a moment, "you can guess the rest." According to Mary, Mike met a man at Harry's Texas Bar. He bought Mike drinks and showed strong interest in the young man's mechanical ability. The next day, Mike's new friend paid him a visit, admired Mike's tools and said that Mike was just the kind of guy he'd been looking for. He offered to bring Mike the repair and maintenance business for his transport company's fleet of sixty-four truck rigs. Mike almost fell over. Here was the answer to all of his problems. Sixty-four truck rigs! Man, what a sweet deal that was. All of a sudden, Mary observed, Mike was busier than a duck chasing Junebugs. His back yard began to resemble a truck stop as the big rigs pulled in and out for repair work.

And it was only a year or so later, Mary added, that unknown to Mike, phase two of his entrapment began. It started with the man who was responsible for bringing Mike the truck business. This time he said he was willing to finance Mike in the expansion of the repair business by building a large, modern repair facility. In that way Mike could enlarge his business and earn more money. He couldn't believe his luck. Little did he know that he was about to pay a price for his good fortune that only the devil could arrange. Payback began, Mary explained, with the sudden withdrawal of the trucking repair business from his new, expensive facility. Without notice or explanation, the big trucks stopped coming to his new garage. Bewildered, anxious to discover if somehow he had offended his customers, Mike suddenly realized he had no way to contact the man he had met at Harry's Texas Bar. Desperate, he canvassed bars and taverns in Chilton, but encountered a wall of silence.

"I think," Mary said, "that Mike was at his lowest point. He knew he'd been a fool, taking his good fortune with a grain of salt, never asking questions, never furnishing himself with a solid reason why a complete stranger would invest thousands of dollars in a mechanic he met casually in a bar.

"Well, wouldn't you know," Mary said with venom in her voice, "Along comes a member of the group at the perfect time when Mike was down and out. Shows up out of the blue with a new proposal for Mike." He told Mike the company needed a driver who could be relied on to do some important pickups and deliveries. For a responsible man like Mike, the rewards could be excellent. Since one hand washes the other, not only would the trucks find their way back to Mike's garage, but the bonus for handling deliveries would be more than generous.

Mary commented that if Mike had questions or concerns about the new deal he never voiced them. He had slipped too far down in his estimation of himself to care about dropping another notch or so. Somehow, the period of deprivation when he'd been cut off from the work and money supply he'd come to depend on, created the perfect state of despair for Sammy, the recruiter of the organization, to make this appearance. Mike started his new job as a well-paid captive of the organization. According to Mary, he enjoyed his good fortune for several years until his curiosity about the crates he was hauling from one place to another prompted him to open one of them. He confirmed what he had suspected: he had been picking up and delivering drugs.

"Well," Mary sighed, "that shook him up. He was furious, felt he'd been deceived. But he continued working for the company, picking up thick envelopes of paperwork and delivering crates of vegetables."

But he developed a small deception of his own, Mary related. In a secret ledger, he began to record his deliveries, the time, the place, the people involved at both ends of the chain. Perhaps he conceived of the idea as a salve to his own bruised ego. Whatever the reason, Mike's decision was the most dangerous thing he'd ever done. His act of deceit, should it have become known, would have resulted immediately in his murder.

"And, of course, " Mary said, shaking her head, "It was he, himself, who bragged about his secret, who wrote his own death sentence. Booze loosened his tongue and his own careless words alerted the company to his treachery." Mary was drawing to the end of her story, and as for myself, my right hand ached from holding the telephone so tightly to my ear.

In an anti-climactic voice, she said, "About two weeks before his death, Mike let the cat out of the bag during a heavy bout of drinking. On one of his frequent visits to Harry's Texas Bar, he talked about his ledger, slyly promising whoever was listening, that with it as evidence, he was going to track his employers and expose their criminal activities.

"God, how stupid, innocent, and dumb he was," said Mary. "How completely he underestimated the people he was involved with. You've got to get up very early in the morning to get the best of them! People who become involved — willingly or not — with them, with that kind of an organization, face an uncertain future. One wrong word, one suspicious act, and they hand out a death sentence without a pause for regret.

"Well, you know the rest," Mary said. "You know his house was ransacked. They were looking for that ledger, but they didn't find it."

Mary was silent for a moment, then with a deep sigh, told me about an abandoned farm house where illegal immigrants were stashed. It was in Chilton. It was a drug house, clearing house and distribution point for Mexicans smuggled over the border. Mary said she could actually show me that house. I knew Mary expected a decision from me. Would I return to Texas, or, aware now of the personal threat to me if I pursued the criminal conspiracy that killed Mike, would I chicken out?

I thought about the danger to me for just a moment, then acknowledged to myself how strongly I wanted to see the farmhouse and the field where Mike met his death. Maybe I could discover evidence that he was drugged before he was killed. I could search for any shred of truth that would establish his homicide.

I thought about the woman who was waiting for my decision. Why had she confided in me? What was her game? Who was she, really? Was it possible for me to trust her? A question without an answer. I informed her I would return to Texas. She told me to be at Harry's Texas Bar between nine and ten o'clock every night.

I sat motionless for a long time after I gave my decision to Mary, aware of the pounding of my heart. What was I letting myself in for? What did I know about investigating a murder? What did I know about playing detective? I guessed that I would have to find out. No matter what I did, it wouldn't bring Mike back. On the other hand, at the very least, I wanted our family to be assured that he didn't kill himself. I doubted that the Chilton Police Department would act on any information I gave to them. The manner in which they had handled the case so far certainly suggested that they might be in the company's pocket. They had been so quick to accept the verdict of suicide when everything pointed to murder. Such an outcome was so convenient for them: suicide — case closed. Well, I wouldn't let it be that convenient. I'd try my best to get to the bottom of Mike's murder.

Of course, I said nothing to my husband Tom about my decision to return to Texas. I knew what his response would be: ridicule, foul language and stinging insults. As a married woman, I lived a pretty solitary life. I confided in no one. Mike and I had been close. Our lives had run parallel courses. He had taken a path that led to self-destruction, and I had to admit that so had I, even if I still refused to recognize the severity of my situation. I still believed that if I could do better, be smarter, be thinner, Tom would not behave in the way he did. His criticisms of me must be justified. The arguments must be my fault. That's okay, I said to myself. I would fix it all when I got back.

Two weeks later, I packed my bag, piled the kids and Red into the van and took off. It would be superfluous for me to report that Tom fought me every step of the way, yelling, screaming, and name calling. I didn't hear him. I tuned him out and left.

When I got to my mother's house in California, I told her about my intention to find out more about the circumstances of Mike's death. I related my conversation with Mary to her and the limited hope she had offered me. Mom listened carefully to my words and I saw her face turn still with fear and concern.

"Don't go there!" she begged. "I think Mary is setting you up, Pam," she insisted. "She's convinced you to come back to Texas, come back to their own backyard. You could end up like Mike," she concluded. Tears gathered in her eyes and spilled down her cheeks.

"Mom, I don't think so. I really don't think so. My conversation with her was genuine. She wants to help me. I'll go, and I'll be all right." Mom kept objecting and she tried a dozen ways to change my mind. In the end, she gathered up the children and their stuff, embraced me tightly for a moment, then I was out the door after hugging my kids goodbye.

"Be good, you guys, " I hollered from the car. "I'll be back soon, and then we'll go home."

I started on my fifteen-hour trip back to the scene of the murder. I wondered what was waiting there for me. Would I discover anything? Would I be in danger? Would Mary be able to help me? The answers to my questions lay in that drab little town of Chilton, a dot on the map; a place that bore an uninteresting history and faced a future as inconsequential as the past. It was certainly a nothing town, perhaps with only the distinction of being a hub of crime, mayhem and murder.

The road stretched before me, a wide ribbon that narrowed and disappeared as it touched the horizon. Trying to catch up with that road was like trying to catch up with the future. I could see nothing but my own past. It was easy for me to slip back into time, and I let my memory play out in the street of my mind.

I had quit college in California, and had taken a job selling pressure-sensitive tape. It was with a large manufacturer that relocated me to New York City. Selling was for me. I was glad that I had discovered a way to make a living that I really enjoyed. My father had taught me how to weld and handle tools and Mom had taught me how to cook and take care of the house. I was well-rounded, fit for life, or so I thought. I loved New York and for the first year I spent every waking moment exploring the most fabulous city in the world. I'm sure I visited every museum and delicatessen. I went to the theatres, walked all over Central Park, attended the ballets and the symphonies, listened to street corner musicians, and watched dancers in Greenwich Village. I ate at great restaurants and at kosher hot dog stands. I had a grand time. What an experience! I liked the people for whom I worked, and I did well selling their product. But, after a couple of steaming, hot and humid summers, my romance with the Big Apple came to an end and I asked my company for a transfer back to the West Coast. I'm a westerner at heart, and I was dying to get back to California.

I pulled off the highway leading east into a service station, filled up with gas, bought a Coke and a bag of nibbles for myself. It seemed my life was married to my van, so much so that I felt I had become part of the old engine's throbs and pulses. I looked at the changing scenes of the countryside. I thought about all the traveling I'd done in my different sales jobs. Tom hated my absence, but loved the paychecks I earned. In the beginning, however, it had all been so different. I remembered when I met him. After three years of working in California after New York, I realized the air was getting as cluttered as the highways, housing developments crowded the land, and life in general was getting too busy, too hectic, and too fast. I dreamt of Oregon. I had visited Portland on several occasions and always regretted leaving the state. I loved everything about that part of the country — the people, the pace, even the rain, and, most of all, the great open spaces and the endless green forests.

It was after I had landed in Portland, that I found a job with a giant lumber company selling corrugated containers. I still chuckled when I recalled the several interviews I had with the Director of Personnel, and how he tried to dominate me, discourage me, and infer strongly that I probably wouldn't be able to do the job.

I finally told him that I wasn't going to put up with his bullshit and his intimidating attitude anymore. "Either you want me, or you don't!" I finally fired at him. "I won't play this game with you anymore. All I know is that I can do the job for you. I can sell. I'm good." I recalled that he laughed at my outburst, and hired me on the spot. And, a good job I did.

Later, I bought some property to the north of Portland.

My brother Mike, who had taken a job with a door manu-facturer nearby, moved in with me. During the time we spent together, I really got to know him. He was a kind and gentle guy. He looked at the world with a grin, enjoyed life, and treated people fair-and-squarely. He brought his friends to the house for meals and visits, and played his guitar, and was interested in a multitude of things. We sat around and talked way into the night about this, that and everything else. He was good company and I never got tired of having him around. Knowing him as he was then made it even harder for me to accept the kind of person he had become, the lifestyle he had chosen, and the sordid, tragic way his life ended, hanging from a cherry picker. Murdered. I'll never forget a philosophical statement he made to me one night while we were exchanging viewpoints: "Baby, the sun will shine," he said to me, "but first the rain must fall." It proved to be a prophecy in his own life, both truthful and sad.

I met Tom after taking a second job in a restaurant in order to save the money to pay cash for some improvements I wanted to make on my property. Tom was a frequent guest at the restaurant where I worked. He was nice — quite a gentlemen. He didn't drink, didn't do drugs, had a steady job with the railroad as a brakeman, and was a devoted outdoorsman. We started going out together and pretty soon he took me out on fishing and hunting trips. It was great! I always loved the outdoors and Tom and I sat around a lot of campfires, camping out, sleeping under the stars. It was a marvelous adventure for me, and I loved it.

Tom took me places I'd never been and I discovered sights and animals I had never seen. I'd never encountered an elk before, until I was transfixed by one who stood like a bronze sculpture in the early morning outlined against a sky growing bright. I saw bears, mountain cats and other creatures in their beautiful wilderness habitat. The outdoor activities fit us both and we made the most of it.

Tom and I talked for hours and we got to know each other. We enjoyed a great love life, and got along like a house on fire. He had a son, Jesse, from his first marriage which ended in divorce. Unfortunately, the animosity between him and his former wife continued and rubbed off on us. Later, Jesse adapted nicely to our lives.

Eventually Tom moved in with me and after three years of being together, we got married, and that's when things changed drastically.

The very first day after our wedding, my husband cut off our sex life. Just like that. At the time I didn't recognize his ultimatum as a control strategy. He told me I was too aggressive, which made him feel like a piece of meat. Strange! He had never complained before. That was the beginning of his program to establish his dominance and my inferiority. The range of his criticisms of me became astonishing:

"I don't like your hair; you're too fat (size four?); I don't like your clothes; the way you talk; the way you cook; keep house; your shoes…your everything!"

I was convinced I needed to make drastic changes to make him happy. I felt responsible for his happiness. Since, obviously, I was the cause of his misery, it would be up to me to make things right. I remembered how I'd felt the same way about my siblings, always taking care of them, always wanting everything to be right for them.

On the other hand, I pondered how I could have become so unattractive and ineffective in such a short time. He had been content and excited with me for three years. I was the same person. I hadn't changed. I was frustrated.

And I had an inkling, even then, that I had created my own hell, and until I was ready to create something better for myself, that was the way it was going to be. But then, I told myself, I loved my husband and I'd make my marriage work!

What puzzled me most was the fact that Tom was an extremely bright man. He could have been anything he wanted to be. He picked up things immediately and never forgot anything he learned. He could have been a surgeon or scientist. He had that kind of mind. But he lost interest in a new idea or endeavor as quickly as he got fired up about it. He was afraid to try new things. Just moving a piece of furniture in our house caused him great stress and brought on an explosion of rage. I learned not to try new foods on him; that too drove him nuts. He felt threatened by anything new and different. He wouldn't attempt anything unique or strange, for fear of failing at it. Therefore, he stagnated, which no doubt added to his frustration.

I'm not a psychologist by any stretch of the imagination, but I was beginning to read a lot, and I learned more and more about human behavior. Sooner or later, I knew I would have to face the fact that I couldn't fix Tom. I could fix myself, but not him. But that time was a long way off, and a lot of drama would have to play out before I had my act together.

Before we were married, I told Tom that according to my doctor I was unable to have children. That was fine with him. He had one son, Jesse, and didn't show any interest in fathering more. But then the odds took a turn. After almost twelve years of marriage, a miracle happened. I was pregnant. My happiness was short-lived. My husband yelled and roared that he didn't want children and told me to get an abortion. I roared back and needless to say, we had a huge, ugly fight but in the end I stuck to my guns. I was going to have the baby. I was almost sorry that I hadn't given in to him when he started to slap our firstborn son, Adam, while he was still in the crib. Tom couldn't stand the baby's crying, and was jealous of the time I spent with our son — time stolen from taking care of his needs. Despite his resentments, his temper, and his punishing ways, we had two more children, another boy and a little girl. And I had to keep interfering with his cruelties. He'd get mad at one of the kids and start spanking, beating, or tossing him or her around. And I would get red-hot and raging.

The only way I could divert his attention away from the kids was to attack him physically. He would let go of his victim, turn on me, and the battle was on. Looking back, I can't believe I lived that way. But I did. After all, I loved him, didn't I?

Strange, I said to myself, how we permit life to repeat when we don't learn the lessons, how when we refuse to read the signs along the way, we fall into the same circumstances with different people. Just like my father, Tom beat his children, tried to batter me, and just like my mother, I was powerless to stop him. Of course, it was inevitable, when I looked back at Tom's behavior, that he would start cheating with other women.

One night, when we were still sleeping together, I knew something was going on. Restless, he got up and said he was taking the car for a drive.

"At this time of night?" I asked, "Where are you going?"

He said, "Why are you asking such a dumb question? I'm going for a drive. I can't sleep, and that's the end of that."

I said, "Why do you want to go out at such a late hour?

And if you are going for a drive, I'll go with you."

"No, " he said. "I just want to go by myself. I want to be alone."

Tom went out and didn't come back that night. My suspicion of his extra-marital affair was confirmed about two weeks later when I discovered a new package of condoms in the pocket of his shirt destined for the wash. One condom was missing. I didn't even bother to confront him with the evidence.

I noticed a "Howdy-Welcome-to-Texas" sign flash by as I drove into the Lone Star State. I stopped at the next roadside café for a bite to eat and to fill the tank with gas. I had decided to drive straight through to Chilton, and get some sleep once I got there. The picture of Mike's body hanging from a thick rope attached high on a cherry picker, superimposed itself upon every thought I had, and directed every decision I made. The all-night roadside café where I stopped was empty and a sleepy waitress seemed glad to break the monotony of her nighttime vigil over the coffee pot. The television above the bar flickered brightly as the images of a late night talk show projected the empty conversation of the celebrity guests whose comments about their careers seemed as trivial as their lives.

The young waitress sauntered over to my table, armed with a coffee pot. Gratefully, I took a sip of the black, steamy fluid and listened to her friendly prattle, of how still the night was, of how lonely her job was, and what was I doing traveling so late at night by myself, and where was I going? When I told her I was going to see my family in Chilton, Texas, she replied that she knew exactly where that was.

"You've still got a long ways to go," she offered, her voice transmitting her concern. A little frown appeared on her forehead. "What a coincidence, " she said. "There was two strange guys here having a few beers. When I asked where they was from, they said Chilton. Those guys were here for a couple of hours, just hanging out by themselves, talking all the time like it was a real private talk. They left out the back way when you came in." I didn't pay much attention to her chatter. After all, everybody's got to be from somewhere.

I finished my meal, sat for a while, let Red out of the van, had it serviced, and headed back out into the dark night. I had traveled only a few miles when I picked up the bright headlights of a vehicle in my rear view mirror. I kept a steady foot on the accelerator and the truck stayed a respectful distance behind me. Suddenly, the vehicle gathered steam, came dangerously close to the rear end of my van, hovered there for a while, fell back, and sped up again. All of a sudden, my heart froze. Hadn't the waitress said something about two men from Chilton? Jesus, God alive, what if they had been waiting for me? What if they were Mike's old friends? What if something had gone wrong? Had Mary talked?

Well, I could be in quite a mess.

I was easy prey, a woman alone, out in the middle of nowhere on a lonely highway wrapped in the black of night. All they had to do was force me off the road, and I would be a goner! I stepped on the gas, picked up speed, and so did the truck. I fell back, and so did the truck. A cold sweat broke out on my forehead and I reached for Red who was curled up in the passenger seat. I wished I could convey my fears to my faithful friend, have him reassure me. Red's head moved reassuringly under my shaking hand. Maybe he was some protection, but even the most faithful dog couldn't stop a bullet. Those Chilton boys didn't fool around. I felt raw and helpless.

I was such a novice at the game of evil and crime.

Watching NYPD Blue on television was about all the education in police work I had. I did have a degree in criminology from Channel Two, but what was that going too get me? Perhaps a bullet between my eyes.

Having traveled this way before, I knew I had more than twenty-five miles to go before I would encounter a sign of human life. There was another café waiting somewhere ahead. My speedometer hovered around eighty, the piercing lights of the pursuing truck lit up my van as it kept pace with me. I started to hum to myself, whistled, finally sang out loud. I had to get my courage up, and finally started to reason with myself and analyze the situation at hand.

Just because these men had told the waitress they were from Chilton didn't mean they lived there, and there was no guarantee that they were connected to the crime ring in any way. Maybe they were just a couple of farm boys, traveling at night, having a little fun with a woman driving by herself. Or, better yet, scaring the hell out of her. Just one of those amusing, self-serving good-old-boy games that they could talk about over a beer at their favorite smoke-filled tavern. Yes, drawing a howling response from their best buddies who would appreciate the image of a woman clutching the wheel of her van in terror. Bastards!

I sang a little louder and prayed silently to myself. Time had no meaning, and I had no idea how long the cruel chase had been going on or how long it would last. My nerves were wearing thin and I started to scream when I saw a faint light in the distance. It must be the café I had expected to see. What if it were closed? It was three o'clock in the morning. As I drew closer to the beckoning lights, I could see in the distance the form of a roadside café. I decided, open or not, I was going to pull off the road and bring my terror to an end — one way or another. As I slowed down for the turn, the pickup with its blinker flashing came around from behind me, honked loudly, and to my great relief, roared past me off into the black, starless night. With my heart beating in my throat, I stopped the van in front of Sam's Prairie Café and Bar next to a couple of dusty, beat up old cars, dropped my head on the steering wheel and went limp.

Terror and gratitude escaped with the rest of my pent up emotions, and I felt like a balloon emptied of air. I let my body sag and waited for my nerve ends to stop shrieking. I sat quietly for a while, avoided thoughts and said a prayer of thanks in hopes of reaching God's ear in case He was listening in on the Texas prairie. I had created a phantom, I had anticipated a danger which had not come to pass and it dissolved like the shadow it was. Then, an ugly "what if" thought opened my eyes wide. What if those men roared off just to make me feel secure, but were waiting by the side of the road, waiting for me to come by, to pick up where they left off? Then, really finish the job? Fresh fear rushed in, making me hot and sweaty all over. I climbed into the back seat of my van, locked the doors, pulled a coat over me and curled up with Red lying protectively at my feet. I'd rest until I saw the light of day, then get a cup of coffee and drive on.

I must have dozed off, for I woke up with a start, trying to figure out where I was. Morning had come with gray skies and more rain. The shadows and phantoms had vanished with the night. I got myself ready to drive on, and was glad that the rest of my trip was uneventful. I arrived at Mike's house tired and weary, but in one piece.

I hated to open the door to the place where he had lived and step back in time. I believe that houses have souls; the walls talk, the rooms convey feelings and hold the secrets of the past. When I occupied Mike's room on my first visit to Chilton, I had been convinced that there were other unseen occupants of the house. I had not changed my mind.

Chapter Six

I arrived at Mike's house, parked the van, and surveyed the front yard. What in the world had happened while I was gone? The yard and house looked deserted and run down even more than when I had first seen them. Neglect showed everywhere. Scraggly grass and weeds peppered the lawn. Papers and trash carelessly left outdoors had been blown here and there by the wind. Old tires, broken plastic buckets and rusted garden tools cluttered up the front porch. Charred, black remnants of what must have been a large bonfire marred the lawn in the backyard. I wondered what had been burned and who had burned it.

I walked up the steps to the porch, sidestepping an accumulation of discarded and broken household bric-a-brac. The front door was unlocked. I turned the knob and walked into the nastiest mess I'd ever seen or smelled in my whole life.

When I stepped into the living room my inclination was to turn and run. On my previous visit to the house, I had cleaned up the clutter left by the Chilton cops when they searched the house shortly after Mike's body was discovered. But someone had come in after I left and had torn the house apart and brutally vandalized it.

The living room looked as if it had died, but no one had bothered to bury it. The sofa pillows had been slashed, shredded and scattered from corner to corner. Books, newspapers and magazines littered the floor. Among shattered knickknacks, small tables lay on their sides, their broken legs sticking into the air accusingly. Pictures had been yanked from their places on the walls, their backs torn open, their glass frames broken, and they leaned at crazy angles against the baseboards. Dirt, mud and glass had been ground into the carpet, along with cigarettes and other unrecognizable shreds of this and that. If the original destruction of the house as a result of the cops' sweeping search of the premises was not bad enough, the apparent viciousness of the second search was like a punishing rape.

Most of the kitchen cupboard doors were torn away, hanging drunkenly on broken hinges. The shelves again had been emptied, the contents flung to the floor. Cereal mingled with loose flour and spilled sugar, noodles and rice, chips and spices. With each of my steps, dried food crunched under my shoes, and black cockroaches scurried to safety. The sink was clogged with filthy dishes and the whole house smelled like a garbage dump. My stomach turned over and I almost lost my lunch. I would have to clean up the mess or set a match to it. I had no alternative; if I was going to stay in the house while I waited to connect with Mary, I'd have to clean it a second time. By restoring order, I might discover another clue to Mike's scheme of retaliation against the gang that had trapped him. After all, I had found a single page from the small daily calendar.

Well, looking at the mess wouldn't make it disappear. I got to work in the living room first. I turned over each piece of paper, book or magazine in my hands. I shook and rattled things; I searched behind the pictures; I checked the couches and the chairs. As I cleaned and restored the living room to a livable condition, leaving the deep stains on the rugs untouched, I handled everything twice, time consuming as it was. Through a veil of booze, Mike had announced to the world that he kept a ledger of his illegal activities. It had to be somewhere. It could have eluded both search parties.

I sat on the one cushion remaining on the couch and briefly surveyed the mountain of trash I had accumulated in one corner of the living room to be hauled outside. I rested for a moment before I had to leave to meet Mary at Harry's Texas Bar. I wasn't concerned that she might not show up on this particular night, but I wasn't going to be late in case she did.

The odors of cigarette smoke and stale beer and the sounds of country music greeted me as I entered Harry's Texas Bar. A tinny voice from the jukebox sang of true love turned bad and two couples clutching each other moved to the slow beat of the music in one far corner. A few solitary figures sat along the bar staring at the television screen and only a few tables had occupants this early in the evening. I didn't see a single woman with blond hair, and headed for an empty dark booth at the back of the tavern. I sat down and waited. A waitress with a sullen expression on her face and a mop of hair that fell to her shoulders poured me a cup of coffee and wiggled her way back to the bar without saying a word.

Two hours, six cups of coffee and a thin ham sandwich later, there was still no sign of Mary. Tired and disappointed, I paid my bill and drove back to Mike's house. I'd cleared the couch that morning in anticipation of sleeping downstairs. For some reason I couldn't explain to myself I felt more control of my life in the living room with Red next to me on the carpet and my stun gun lying beside me.

The next morning I attacked the kitchen and virtually repeated the cleaning routine that I had practiced when I had occupied the house after Mike's funeral. I had just finished when I heard the lock in the front door turn.

It was Dawn-Lee who stepped into the living room, not at all pleased to see me. When I asked her what she knew about the bonfire in the backyard she replied defensively that she had burned some "stuff." Her tone of voice clearly conveyed her resentment of my presence. After all, she whined, she was a widow and I had invaded her territory. Her once pretty face was rough and blotchy; she was dressed carelessly, her hair stringy and unkempt.

When I told her that I had returned to try and find the truth about the circumstances of her husband's death, she only shrugged her shoulders, looked at me without a flicker of interest, barely mumbled a goodbye and left. I watched her get into her car and drive off without a backward glance. I realized how little I knew about the woman Mike had married. Not only were we separated by distance, but by loyalties, ideals and desires.

Yes, we were strangers. I thought I had known my own brother well because we were siblings, and as adults had shared a house for a while. But that hadn't counted. I realized that I had idealized Mike, giving him credit for qualities and a richness of character that I wanted him to have, but which, unfortunately, he had not developed. I could see that that was also true of my relationship with Tom, my husband. He was not the man I wished him to be; his reality and the person I had sculptured in my imagination to be my mate were as different as night and day. Stubbornly, I had clung to my made-up version of who Tom should be through sixteen years of marriage and I ended up almost hating him because he refused to be the person I created him as.

I was fascinated with the relevance of my sudden understanding; it was as if a bright light had gone on in my head, and I remembered a passage I had found intriguing when I read Willa Cather in college:

"Sometimes a neighbor whom we have disliked a lifetime for his arrogance and conceit lets fall a single commonplace remark that shows us another side, another man; a man uncertain, puzzled, and in the dark like ourselves."

Uncertain and puzzled — that was Mike, and me as well, and Tom.

That night I returned to Harry's Texas Bar and again was disappointed with the failure of Mary to show up.

The next night I arrived at Harry's Bar earlier and had barely settled into my booth at the far end of the tavern when a slender blond woman came through the door. She wore light tan cotton slacks that fit her trim figure perfectly, topped by an expensive–looking black silk shirt, and she carried a huge leather purse slung over one shoulder. When the door swung shut behind her, she looked around, surveying the room. When her eyes caught mine, I nodded my head slightly and she walked directly to my booth. As she came closer, I saw that she was quite a bit taller than I, and carried herself with assurance and purpose. She stopped at my table, looked at me and said, "Pam?" I nodded and she slid quickly into the booth opposite me without a word. She moved against the far wall, away from the light that hung over the table.

"I'm sorry I couldn't make it sooner, " she said with the husky voice I remembered from our long phone call. "I had to be sure the boys were all out of town on their errands before I could show up here. I had to make certain I wouldn't be seen with you." With that, Mary dropped her big purse on the seat next to her, reached inside and retrieved a pack of cigarettes and a slim gold lighter.

She ordered a beer from the waitress who had come by, proceeded to light a cigarette, leaned her head way back and slowly blew the smoke into the air. "Sorry," she smiled apologetically, "I still have the habit."

She was an attractive woman in her early thirties, I judged, with high cheekbones, big brown eyes, thick long lashes and silky blond hair that lay smooth like a cap over her head. Her hands were manicured and well groomed, her makeup subtle and flawless. She wore two heavy gold bracelets on one wrist, and an expensive gold and diamond "status" watch on the other. Her earrings were made of single large pearls set in simple circles of gold. Not for a moment did she look as if she belonged in a hick town like Chilton. She was New York or San Francisco.

"I'm glad you came." Keeping my voice low, I looked straight at her. "I was going to leave tomorrow if you didn't show up tonight. I really didn't know what to do."

Mary took a deep breath, frowned, shook her head from side to side as though questioning her sanity for sitting with me, and gestured with her hands across the table as if to touch me.

"You know, maybe I shouldn't have come. If I've learned anything, I've learned that you can't keep a secret in this business. I know that for a fact. There's a hell of a lot I could tell you, and a hell of a lot more I can't, and won't. You're as naive as your brother. Have you any idea how powerful and far-reaching these people are? We're not talking about a bunch of small town crooks; these are big time operators as savvy and as sophisticated as any of the boys in the big cities. Hanging out here in the middle of nowhere is simply a matter of convenience, not a sign of being small and dumb."

I decided it was time to put some steel in my voice.

"I don't really care about the pedigrees of these hoodlums. I want to know about my brother. I know he didn't commit suicide, and I want to find some proof of it. Also, let's be frank about why you're here. It isn't out of charity. You hope to gain some advantage from what you tell me and how I put it to use."

Mary looked at me with surprise in her eyes. "I'm sorry if I came on too strong. But even if you could prove your brother was murdered, and even if the police were straight arrows, you can't touch them. That's impossible. If you tried, you'd lose. You are right about one thing. I do hope to find an advantage in the stir you make. I know you're wondering what the hell a nice girl like me is doing in a situation like this. Well, that's another story I may tell you one day, but not now. You've got to trust me."

For just a moment, I caught a fleeting look of deep fear in Mary's eyes and I detected old lines of regret around her mouth. Despite her surface hardness, I knew I was face to face with a miserable, desperate young woman.

To impress on me how ruthless the gang was, Mary brushed the hair out of her face in a typical gesture and told me about a man who had been working for the organization for several months when he spooked and made discrete noises about wanting to get out. He tried to convince his boss that his family on the East Coast needed him, that his mother was ailing and his father required his support. He built a strong case for himself, but failed to move his boss. When he became more insistent that he must have his freedom, his boss authorized a demonstration to change his mind.

It was to happen on an outing to which the man and his five-year-old boy were invited for a little Sunday fishing. It would take place at a remote area in the hills where the boss had a cabin next to a lake.

"Listen, Mark," he said, "Why don't you and that boy of yours come on out for an afternoon of fishing. We can talk some more then. There's some great trout in Diamond Lake. I stocked it myself. I'll have a couple of the fellas join us. We'll rustle up some barbeque, drink some beer, and have a few laughs, then we'll talk. Leave the little woman at home. Just bring your boy and we'll make it an all man day," he said jovially, slapping Mark on the back.

Thirty-four-year-old Mark Pettit had been in financial difficulties when he met with the "boss" and in no time at all that obliging, friendly gentleman arranged for his release from a dead end job and found a way to make him debt-free. Also, these gifts tied him securely to the apron strings of the operation. Unlike his friend Mike, Mark knew what he was getting into, but like other people who had been recruited, was certain that if he did a good job for awhile, after he had earned the trust of his supervisors, they'd eventually let him go his own way. Naive reasoning! The first time he asked to be relieved of this job, he was marked for a demonstration.

When Mark arrived at the lake with his bright and active five-year-old son, he met two other men who belonged to the organization. Neither one seemed to have been given a last name. They were known only as the Gold Dust Twins, Sammy and Willy.

Sammy was tall and wiry with a mean–looking, acne scarred face. A few thin black hairs on his chin which would never grow into a beard, and an equally poor showing of hair under his nose, gave him an unfinished appearance. His habit of squinching one eye shut when he talked as if to better zero in on what he saw was disconcerting. Also, whenever he wanted to stress a point of conversation, he punched his right fist into his outstretched left hand like a catcher at a baseball game. His total appearance suggested a mean streak which he enjoyed displaying to intimidate people.

Willy, on the other hand, was tall and solid, with a powerful set of shoulders and arms. His faded cowboy shirt strained over his muscled upper body and was tucked snugly into his well-worn jeans. There was no wasted flesh on Willy; he was all muscle. His deeply tanned face had the calm, broad passivity of his Russian peasant stock. A shock of wiry red hair gave him a boyish look, but his dark brown eyes were unfriendly and cold.

Nasty as Sammy was, Willy was the dangerous one. He had the muscle and he had the smarts. The two were an unbeatable pair.

In the company of Mark and the boss, the two men hoisted a few beers. Mark's son Jimmy took a paper cup filled with Coke and ice to the lakeshore less than thirty feet away from the adults, where he settled down to dig in the wet sand. During his conversation with the boss, Willy, and Sammy, Mark rambled on about leaving his job with the organization and moving east to help with his family grocery store. The longer he talked, the quieter his boss got. He finally broke in and asked, "In other words, Mark, old buddy, there ain't nothing we can do to keep you?"

"No hard feelings, Boss," Mark replied. "I'm not ungrateful for what you've done for me, and I'll pay you back with interest every cent before I leave, but I've got to be there for my folks. And," he added gratuitously, "You know me. I won't talk. I know how to keep my mouth shut." With that he rested his case.

The boss noted the determination on Mark's face, then nodded to Sammy and Willy, as if in acknowledgment of the logic in Mark's argument. With this sign, Sammy slowly got to his feet from his lawn chair, strolled leisurely to his parked Jeep, got in, started the motor, and slowly guided the vehicle in a half circle so that the front end was pointed at the lake where little Jimmy was absorbed with building a fort on the frontier out of sand from the beach.

Sammy waved his arm negligently at Mark and the two other beer drinkers, raced the Jeep's motor and aimed the vehicle at Jimmy.

Mark, white-faced with sudden terror, yelled, "No!" as the Jeep, traveling in a straight line, struck his son with a sickening thump and catapulted the boy's body forty feet in an arc over the lake that ended with a splash in the water.

Madness, shock and grief burned in Mark's eyes as he ran to the water's edge and waded toward the spot where his son's body had sunk.

"Help me, somebody, help me!" He plunged forward and was already hip deep in the water when Sammy and Willy grabbed him firmly, pulled him back on the shore and threw him face down on the sand. They pinioned him, keeping him stationary until the surface of the lake was still again, without ripples, and there was no sign of Jimmy's body. They pulled the father erect and he stood staring at the lake with tears running down his cheeks, like a drunk swaying in the wind. When he finally turned away, his eyes were dead, like burned holes in a blanket, and his face mirrored an empty world.

Never again in the years to follow did Mark ever renew his request to leave the company. He told his wife that their son had drowned and all attempts to find him had failed. Just a few months later, she left her husband and returned to the East where her parents lived.

"Yes," Mary said in a small voice, "Mark's still here; he's working for the Man. "Now, do you understand a little better what you're up against? Do you still want to hear how Mike died, or have you had enough?"

I swallowed hard to push back the bile that had risen in my throat. Kill a child to keep the father in line? Murder an innocent boy to insure his parent's loyalty? A sob caught in my throat and I could barely breath. What kind of barbarism was this? How could they get away with murder? Poor Mike, stupid little grown-up boy who didn't have a chance. Where did justice fit into a scheme of things that permitted hired killers to function as servants of death, to enforce a fear-driven code of compliance to anarchy? I was stunned, an innocent whose eyes had been forced open to witness the true dark side of the human soul. It was not pretty.

Mary looked at me strangely and went on, "Just like the little boy, your brother was murdered. I already told you that. I think now I should tell you how it was done."

I was afraid to hear about Mike now, but I had to process the grief and anger to arrive at an ultimate settlement with his killers, whatever that might be. I wanted to hear it all, and I wanted it to be over. I wanted to get out into the fresh air and look at the vastness of the night sky. I wanted to feel sheltered and loved. I wanted to hug my children, but first, I needed to place Mike's ending in a realistic perspective. I wanted to know about his death.

Mary took a deep drag on her cigarette. Her face was serious and the frown line between her eyes deepened in concentration. This was the story she told me:

When Mike's drinking got worse and he shot off his mouth in public, making all of his stupid threats, the decision was made to get rid of him. And of course, the executioners chosen were Sammy and Willy, who showed up one night at Harry's Texas Bar in their worn blue jeans, faded cotton shirts and down-at-the-heels cowboy boots. Sammy and Willy joined Mike at his table, joking with him, as if they had no other thought on their minds. Mike had been drinking for several hours when the predators insisted he have another beer with them. Sammy and Willy joked around and laughed with Mike, and amid convivial back slapping and buddy talking beckoned to the waitress to drop off a pitcher of ice cold beer. Sammy poured and Willy put a guiding hand on Mike's shoulder, turning him halfway around to face the tavern door, to focus his attention on a couple who were arguing loudly. While Mike was distracted, Sammy pulled two small vials from his pants pocket and dropped their contents into Mike's beer.

After observing the feuding twosome at the tavern door for a moment, amused by their petty squabbling, Mike resumed his position at the table and took a healthy swig of his fresh beer. Sammy encouraged him to drink up, so they could all go to another place for more fun. Mike drained his glass, then sat for a moment, and kept pinching his eyes shut and shaking his head as though to rid himself of something unpleasant.

Sammy and Willy put their arms around his shoulders, and with Mike firmly supported between the two of them, marched out of the tavern. They were in a jolly good mood and played the good-old-boy, best-buddy routine to the hilt. Their boisterous laughter could be heard clearly in the dark night.

Mary halted her narrative and asked me, "Do you really want me to go on? Here comes the bad part. Willy told me all about it later on."

I nodded my head a little and I couldn't get a word out. According to Mary, the three men piled in Sammy's big black pickup and roared off into the night.

Sammy drove about twenty miles out of town to a lonely spot overgrown with wild bushes that lined a farmer's field, pulled the truck behind some shrubs away from the road, yanked the unprotesting Mike out of the front seat. Sammy must have given Mike a hell of a big dose because he had trouble walking; his knees kept buckling. His assailants grasped his arms on either side and dragged him a hundred feet or so off the road as if he were a sack of potatoes.

The men released their burden in the dusty field, with Mike mumbling some garbled words of protest. On the ground, Mike's body relaxed in the thrall of the drugs he had been given, and he was quickly turned face down in the dirt. He tried to raise himself with his outstretched hands but was unable to move his torso. He groped feebly in the dust with his fingers, dimly aware that something was wrong; he shouldn't be lying in the dirt. Impatient to execute the homicide, Sammy stepped on one of Mike's hands with his boot and watched Willy lower himself onto his victim's back. When Mike reared up, trying to shake the weight of Willy off of his back, the man secured his position by straddling Mike's back and with his huge hands, forced Mike's face into the earth.

There was only minimum light to guide the killers, for the night was without a moon. The wind had risen and had brought a chill to the air. Willy, perched on Mike's back, reached into his back pocket and pulled out a plastic bag. With one hand, he lifted Mike's head off the ground just far enough to slip the bag over his head, gathered the ends of the thin plastic tightly behind his victim's head and twisted the open end of the bag into a tight knot. He held on tightly, maintaining the pressure of his knees on his victim's back, as Mike struggled feebly.

When Mary related this particular portion of the homicide, I gasped and wrapped my arms around myself, rocking back and forth. I trembled from head to foot and felt cold sweat breaking out all over my body. I couldn't believe my ears! Mary's account of my brother's death was an exact replica of the nightmare that drove me out of my bed in Idaho weeks ago. Down to the last detail, it was my dream all over again. It had been a tell-tale forecast of the future.

I knew Willy's face though I had never seen him in person. From the vivid picture in my mind, I saw him pull the plastic bag over Mike's head. I knew I would never forget the murderous expression that consumed Willy's face with an evil that glorified the blackness of death. My original vision of Mike's bulging eyes and his protruding tongue as he gasped for breath returned to stab my heart with a wound that was deeper than sin.

In a voice that I hardly recognized as my own, I said to Mary, "You will probably think I'm crazy, but in a dream a month or so ago, I say Mike lying in the dirt, face down. I saw the man, the plastic bag, I saw everything. I tried to scream, I tried to warn Mike, but no sound came from my throat. I saw Mike's face distorted and red with his tongue hanging out of his mouth. Everything you described, I saw before."

Mary eyes flew open; she stared at me over the rim of her beer glass. "You're kidding. You mean you had a dream, saw your brother killed? Jesus, that's weird. You some kind of a psychic?"

"No! I don't know what I am."

Mary looked at her watch, shook her head and said with a touch of impatience in her voice, "I'm sorry, Pam. Let me finish and get this over with; I've got to go, and there's not much else to tell."

"Willy pushed himself off of Mike's unmoving body, looked at the dead man for any lingering signs of life, then watched as Sammy swung his right arm in a wide arc and hurled the two small glass vials into the stubble which covered the field.

Sammy protested when Willy asked him to lend a hand to lift Mike's body from the ground onto the floor of the pickup.

"Why in the hell do you want to do that? We'll cover him with some brush and leave him here. Ain't nobody ever comes out here this time of year. Let the buzzards and coyotes find him and finish him off. Ain't gonna be nothing left of him but his bones come plowing time."

"Shut up and do as I tell you," Willy hissed. "We're going to take him back to his house and make his death look like a suicide. You ought to know better than to leave the body here. Stupid, don't you ever watch the news? There's always some damn kids snooping around, chasing a rabbit, doing something wild that will cause them to stumble on the body. They always do."

The two men argued back and forth. "How in the hell are you going to make it look like suicide? He's filthy, he's covered with dirt. Sure don't look to me like he died in his bed," Sammy groused.

"Just shut up and help me throw him in the truck. We'll clean him up later," Willy said through clenched teeth. "I know what to do. Mike's got a small cherry picker in his garage. We're going to get a piece of rope, hoist him up, and hang him from it. We'll leave the ladder so it looks like he jumped off to do the job. That's all there is to it. Come on, man, let's go do it."

With that, Willy grabbed Mike's feet and reluctantly Sammy grasped Mike's body under the shoulders, and on Willy's count of three, the men heaved the heavy body onto the steel floor in the back of the pickup.

Sammy climbed into the passenger side of the pickup cursing under his breath. Willy paid no attention to his troublesome partner's complaint. He was used to hearing him spout off, often calling him a goddam gas bag and worse.

Willy turned on the motor and raced the engine for a moment to irritate Sammy, then drove off in a spurt of dust. Sammy pushed the button to turn on the radio and grinned to himself over the words in a country-and-western song that twanged of betrayal, treachery and revenge.

It was about one o'clock in the morning when Willy guided the pickup into Mike's neighborhood. In his haste to complete the rest of the job and not attract attention, he had been driving with the lights off. He almost overshot the house, braking sharply and cursing the squealing tires as the truck fishtailed into the driveway, coming to a halt inches away from the front of the garage. Willy turned off the motor and the men remained seated for a minute to make certain that their noisy arrival hadn't awakened anyone in the neighborhood.

Quickly, Willy walked through the gate joining the house and the garage and found the ladder he was looking for. Guarding the beam of a small flashlight he held in his hand with the other, he removed the ladder from its hook on the wall. Despite his caution he and Sammy made noises as they lifted Mike's body out of the truck and carried it into the garage. First, they opened the big service door that swung on hinges up to the garage ceiling. Next, they tied a clothesline around Mike's neck and hoisted him partially into an erect position, then secured the other end of the rope, with several feet of slack, to the arm of the cherry picker. They were both disappointed and disgusted when they let go of Mike's body and it sunk down almost to the floor.

As an afterthought, Willy directed the beam of the flashlight over the tools on the wall and located a small bristle brush. He applied it vigorously to the dust on Mike's clothes, then tossed it aside.

"Let's get out of here," he grunted, and they drove off more quietly than they had come.

When Mary had concluded her narrative, she sighed and said, "Look, Pam, I'll say it one more time. Your brother is dead. Nothing you can do will bring him back. You know the local police aren't going to do anything. They've got their own agenda and have closed the case. All you can do is end up dead. And I'm serious. The guys who run the gang know you've been snooping and I wouldn't be surprised if you've been followed."

Mary sat and fidgeted for a few more minutes, then briefly described the location of what she referred to as the "killing field" and suggested that if I insisted on being crazy, I might want to look in the field for the empty vials that contained the drug used to dope Mike.

Also, she described the location of the old abandoned farmhouse she had referred to in our telephone conversation, the one she said was used as a way station for Mexican illegals and a drug distribution point.

"You can't miss it," she said. "It's an old drab-looking place. A real has-been frontier type farmhouse. It looks like the roof has been pulled down over the porch; that's how steep it is. The porch sags, the lean-to on the north side is about ready to cave in, and the weeds in the front yard are as tall and as thick as shrubs. There are three weather-worn old wagon wheels that lean against the rusty mailbox. Its flag is stuck in a permanent up position. Somebody tried to paint a bunch of black-eyed Susans on the mailbox. You'll see, you can't miss it," she assured me.

"Well, I guess that's it," she said, looking at me quizzically with her lovely brown eyes. "Don't do anything dumb. Take care."

I detained her for just a moment with a question I'd asked her before and had never received a satisfactory answer to.

"Why have you shared all these deadly secrets with me? Aren't you afraid of the same fate as Mike? What do you hope to gain by helping me?"

Mary remained silent for a moment, then said softly, "I liked Mike. Maybe it was more than that. I never shared my feelings with him, but I was working myself up to it. I had a dream about us running away together. It probably wouldn't have worked out."

She paused, picked up her shoulder bag from the bench where we were sitting, pulled the strap over her shoulder, rose to her feet and said, "I told you when we first started talking that there were things I couldn't and wouldn't explain. That hasn't changed. If I were you, I'd watch my back and plan all my moves as if my life depended on it. Because it does."

I sat a few minutes longer in my booth wondering what my next step should be. Every word Mary had used to describe Mike's brutal murder matched the death scene images I had dreamed. Now, I wished I could drum up a vision of the next few days. Mary had warned me to plan all of my moves as if my life depended on it. I believed her. In view of her warning, I had to decide how great the risk would be for me to investigate the killing field. Also, even if I found the glass vials Sammy and Willy had used to drug Mike, how could I use them?

All of a sudden, I was exhausted, weary, depressed and unable to think. I decided it was time for me to head back to Mike's house and curl up on the battered sofa with Red at my feet.

Chapter Seven

The house felt damp and chilly and the air was muggy when I woke up the next morning. I looked out the window and wasn't surprised to see fat, gray wind-whipped clouds sailing by at a fast clip. Rainwater had accumulated on the sagging steps of the front porch overnight, puddles had formed on the lawn, and the ugly, wide cracks and holes in the cement walks had turned into miniature lakes. It was wet everywhere. The heavy rain had slowed down to a steady, fine drizzle that clung to the world like a wet shroud. I thought about my plans for the day, and wished for Texas sunshine.

Before we had parted last night at the tavern, Mary had given me directions to the old farmhouse and to what she called the killing field. I was going to both places today to look around for anything that could pass as evidence in the murder of my brother. For a moment I thought of myself, a fool on an impossible quest. What did I think I could accomplish? What could I find in an open field where a murder had taken place more than four weeks ago? Sun and rain, wind and weather all could have easily erased any pertinent signs or clues in that length of time. Was I looking for a needle in a haystack? Well, as long as I believed there was a needle, I had to keep looking. But then, where would I take evidence if I found something incriminating? No, not to the local cops, but I couldn't conceive of law enforcement authorities at other levels of jurisdiction ignoring a major crime. Also, there were always the newspapers, whose influence could open an investigation.

I put aside the question of where to take my findings.

I had talked my brother Stewart into coming along with me. He had been not only reluctant to get involved with my project, but at first was furious that I should invite him on the strength of our familial ties to jeopardize the secure and placid course of his life. An ex-marine, Stewart had served with distinction in the Desert Storm war, winning a Silver Star for bravery in action and a Purple Heart for the wound that was responsible for his discharge. My personal opinion was that Stewart, like many veterans who had survived the battlefield, was horrified by the idea of exposing himself to danger again, no matter what the venue or reason for the jeopardy. He finally gave in and accompanied me as a token presence. He wasn't convinced that my motive made any sense at all.

"You're just looking for trouble, Sis," he objected. "Let it rest. Those guys killed Mike in cold blood. What do you think they'll do to us if they discover we're on to something? Invite us to a tea party? We'll be out there in a Godforsaken open field, unprotected and vulnerable. What if they follow us? If we're caught snooping around, then we've had it. They can get rid of us right there, and nobody'll ever know. These guys are no amateurs, they play for keeps," he argued. "Besides," he added stubbornly, "It won't bring Mike back."

How many times had I heard that remark and ignored it?

"Hey, Stew, what happened to that tough ex-marine? Don't tell me it's too hot for you. If I dare go, so can you," I cajoled and pleaded until he finally gave in. I told him I'd pick him up by nine o'clock in the morning.

I pulled up in front of his house right on time. I just had to honk once and Stew came out of the house and got into the van. He barely said good morning to me and didn't look very happy. He mumbled something about hoping I wouldn't have to regret my decision to pursue Mike's killers. He had a lousy attitude which didn't help me at all. I had so little to go on and needed all the support I could get.

"Oh, well," I said, "you know what they say, 'No guts, no glory.' Let's go!"

We both wore old jeans, heavy boots and rain jackets with hoods attached. Always the optimist, I had brought along gloves for picking up things, and plastic bags to store the "evidence." Mary had hastily sketched something like a map on a paper napkin in the tavern, and I looked at the scraggly lines, trying to figure out were I was supposed to go. I followed the main highway out of town for about eight miles until I came to a Y in the road. The crude map indicated a right turn onto a county road, which would lead to the killing field after another twelve miles or so. She had made a fat X on the thin paper next to a tall, lonely tree she had drawn. She told me I couldn't miss the old oak because it was the only one sitting at the edge of the field for miles. That was the killing field.

Stewart and I drove in an uncomfortable silence toward our destination. How different he was from the curious, energetic boy he had been, who couldn't keep his nose out of any situation that offered intrigue or a different path to follow. Every few minutes, he turned his head to see if anyone was following us. I had told him that Sammy and Willy, the gang's hit men, drove a black pickup truck, and they would be the most likely ones to keep an eye on me. I should have just kept my mouth shut. Stewart was nervous and jittery, and I knew he wished he were somewhere else — anywhere.

We came to the Y indicated on my makeshift map, which was easily recognizable. I turned and bumped along on the narrow, rough dirt road. My brother, who had furtively looked over his shoulder most of the way, seemed satisfied no one was following us, and relaxed a bit. The road ran in a straight, rain-soaked ribbon along wheat fields that had long been harvested, and their short stubble stretched as far as I could see under the gloomy sky.

After twenty minutes a shape appeared on the left side of the road, and as I drew closer it turned into a tall, rounded oak tree. I slowed the van and pulled up beside the old oak that must have been there for a hundred years. It was huge. I looked around, and as Mary had promised, I couldn't have missed it. There wasn't another tree in sight, and besides that, the thick bushes that ran for several hundred feet at the edge of the field fit Mary's description of the murder scene to perfection. My heart started to pound, and I felt that familiar blend of fear and excitement rise in my throat that I had experienced a lot lately. It kept me going.

There had not been a solitary sign of another vehicle ever since I turned onto the country road, and I felt safe

from discovery. I pulled off the road, drove onto the field
through a narrow opening between the bushes and the tree,
steered to my left, and stopped behind the wall of greenery
that would hide our presence from anyone passing by.

"Well," I turned to my brother, who sat motionless
next to me staring out the window, "here we are. Let's give
it our best shot and see what we can find."

Stewart turned to me. "You go ahead," he said, his
voice sullen, "You know what you're looking for. I'm not
going to move from where I'm sitting. I told you I didn't
want to have anything to do with this, and not only that," he
continued crossly, "but look where you parked. You're in
deep mud. We'll probably get stuck, and won't be able to
drive out."

My heart sank. He was right. I got out of the car and
my boots sank into the rain-soaked field. The tires of the
van sat in mud almost up to the hubcaps, and that could
mean trouble. Later, I thought, later.

"I can't do anything about that right now, and I'm not
leaving the van parked on the road," I mumbled under my
breath as I banged the door shut behind me, and I proceeded
to walk into the field. Mud clung to my boots, and my feet
made a slushy, sucking sound with each step. I stopped and
let my eyes wander. In the far distance, off to my right at
least 500 yards, I saw a copse of trees that could possibly be
a homestead. Nothing else cluttered the landscape. Dismal
gray land stretched before my eyes until it merged with the
gray horizon and disappeared.

My breath caught in my throat. I felt odd, standing
near the spot where my brother had lost his life at the hands
of two ruthless killers who had asphyxiated him on the
whim of some unknown "boss." I looked at the imprints my
heavy boots left in the earth, and for a moment I was

grateful for the rain. I could see where I had walked and would avoid going around in circles.

I remembered Mary's words that Sammy and Willy had gone about one hundred feet into the field with Mike propped up between them before they dropped him to the ground for the kill. With my eyes glued to the terrain, I slowly walked away from the van, counting my steps. When I figured I had gone a hundred feet or more, I stopped. Wet clumps of earth cluttered the field, small hills and valleys formed random patterns with rivulets of water running between them. I turned, took one long step to my left, and following the footprints to my right, went back the way I had come. For the next hour I went back and forth, leaving rows and rows of footsteps up and down the field, my eyes glued to the wet, brown earth. I changed directions and walked to the right of my first steps and scoured the earth for anything that didn't belong there.

I was just about ready to call it quits when I saw something foreign glistening in the brown earth. I bent down, and my heart jumped. Resting against a clump of dirt was a small vial, the kind that could easily have contained pills or a powder — drugs! The cap was off, but that didn't worry me. I pulled one of the plastic baggies out of my pocket, dropped in my find, and zipped it shut. With my eyes riveted to the ground, I looked for the second vial. Mary had told me that Sammy threw away two vials which had contained the drugs used to paralyze Mike. Trying to figure out the radius in which the killer may have tossed the small containers, I walked in a circle, enlarging it with every other step. That second little bottle had to be right around the spot where I had found the first one.

I came across the other vial within minutes. I almost stepped on it before I retrieved it from its muddy resting place. This one had the cap still on, but was as empty as the first one. I added it to its mate. I wondered what had been in them, what kind of drugs — not that it mattered. Finding the vials could confirm what had been hearsay up to now. Mike had been drugged. Well, I thought, everything leaves a residue, especially pills or powder. A good forensic specialist could identify whatever these vials had contained, and perhaps find fingerprints on the glass.

My eyes swept the vast expanse of the field one more time, as though saying farewell to my brother. I knew I would never return. I closed the book on that. Slowly, I walked back to where I had left Stewart and Red, who were probably tired of waiting in the van. I was within a few feet of my car when a quarrelsome voice bellowed at me from my right. I whirled, my heart in my mouth, and saw the angry figure of a man cradling a shotgun in his arms emerge from behind the tall bushes. My mouth was dry when he yelled at me from no more than thirty feet away.

"What in the hell are you doing hanging around in my field? This is private property, and I don't want people stomping around here," his gruff voice announced, and at the same moment relief and gratitude washed over me as I realized his aggravation was not fatal. I could have hugged the old guy. I wasn't looking at a killer, just a farmer investigating a trespasser.

"Oh," I tried to appear cool, "just looking around. I thought I saw a big dog chase something, and I stopped to look. I love animals," I ventured, "and I'm always curious what goes on in nature. Could I have seen a deer?" I looked questioningly at him, hoping he wouldn't study the wavering lines of footprints I had left in the mud.

"Could've been. There's all sorts of critters scampering around out here," the old man replied, letting his gun drop a bit.

"Well, I didn't mean to trespass on your land. No harm done. I'd better be on my way. It's awfully wet out here." I quickly said goodbye, knocked some of the mud off my boots, climbed into my van, and hoped to God I could get the damn thing out of the mire without any trouble.

Stewart surprised me; his face was pale. Fear? "I heard voices," he said, "I was about to drive off and leave you. I thought you'd stay out there forever."

"I found what I came for," I said quickly, starting the engine, slowly backing up. After a moment's hesitation, the wheels gripped firmly, the mud flew away from the tires in a spray, and we rolled safely onto the road. I breathed a sigh of relief as I turned my vehicle around and headed back in the direction from which we had come. I felt a slight glow of satisfaction that I had found what I had come for. What a stroke of luck, I thought jubilantly to myself. Acres and acres of land, and I found two tiny bits of plastic in the soggy earth. I took it for a good sign. Perhaps I was destined to accomplish what I had set out to do — point the finger at Mike's killers.

"I want you to take me home," Stewart said. "I don't want to go looking for that damn farmhouse or anything else. I've had enough. This isn't gong to take you anywhere but into trouble. Give it up. Quit!"

I reached into my pocket, pulled out the plastic bag and dangled it in front of him. "See what I found? These are the little bottles Sammy tossed into the field after they killed Mike. They contained the drugs they used on Mike. I'm going to have them analyzed and checked for fingerprints by a forensic laboratory."

My brother dismissed my discovery with a wave of his hand, looked at me unhappily and shook his head. "So, you prove these plastic containers contained drugs. But how are you going to demonstrate they were the drugs Sammy dropped into Mike's beer? Mike's autopsy report did not mention drugs. Second, even if they do find fingerprints, they just may be ones the F.B.I. has no records of. What's that going to help? How are you going to connect all this so-called evidence to the killers? You'll never even get to those two goons, but Sammy and Willy may get to you!

"I'm not going to the local police with all that," I interrupted, "I'll go to the F.B.I."

"Let's just drop it," he shot back at me. "We're not going to solve anything. Not now, not ever," he predicted. "I really don't want to argue. I know it means a lot to you. But you're going about it like a kid chasing a butterfly without a net. You're not catching anything, just spinning your wheels, wasting time and money."

I reached over to pat his hand. I didn't want to quarrel with him. We were two people with different ideas about life and dreams. I felt sorry for him and the boy with adventure in his smile that Stewart once was. I guess we die in a lot of ways.

"It's okay, Stewart. I don't know what the outcome will be. All I know is that I'm going to follow up on one more thing, and then I'll go home. I could say I'll never rest until our brother's killers are found and punished, but I don't think that's real. You know me, you know how stubborn I am, how I cling to my goals, how tenacious I am when I want to see something through. And I still have a way to go before I throw in the towel."

Stew nodded in silence, and when we drove up to his house, he gave me a quick pat on the shoulder and went on his way. I took myself to the nearest eatery, ordered a sandwich and black coffee; my mind was racing.

Here I was, in a little, no-way-out town in central Texas few people ever heard of, and which I suspected was controlled by members of a highly sophisticated international criminal ring whose network stretched across several countries. This organization was heavily involved in drug trafficking and the smuggling of illegal immigrants into the United States. And I was going to put a crimp in their operations? I had to admit that Stewart's cynicism was more practical than my idealism.

My stubborn streak won out; I was going to look at that farmhouse. Who knows....

I finished my lunch, got back behind the wheel of my mud-splashed van, and with Mary's directions in my mind, went looking for the farmhouse. I didn't know who and what I was going to find when I got there, and neither had I thought of a good explanation for my presence, should I run in to someone. I'd have to play it by ear.

On this drive, I headed east out of Chilton searching for the road signs Mary had mentioned. Sure enough, I came upon the small bridge that led over Millard's Creek. As directed, I took the fork exactly three miles later, and ended up on a soggy, bumpy no-maintenance dirt road that hugged the land on either side. Every once in a while I came across small herds of cattle grazing, which added a bucolic touch to the flat landscape. I came across a cluster of outbuildings and a house far off to the left of me, but when I reached the dirt road that led to the place there was no sign of a mailbox or a collection of old wagon wheels.

But then I was there. Leaning crazily to one side, ready to fall over for good, there was the mailbox sporting some splashes of fading yellow on one side, a memory of the hand-painted black-eyed Susans. Several wagon wheels rested at the base of the mailbox at odd angles. My eyes surveyed the narrow road and came to rest on what appeared to be a big, run-down house with the kind of deeply sloping roof line Mary had described to me. I turned slowly off the main road and bumped and sloshed towards the building. There was no sign of man or beast to be seen when I pulled up in front of the sagging porch. Piles of junk, rusty tools, crumpled fenders, parts of an old washing machine, half a truck bed, a dead tractor on one wheel, and several wooden crates lay where they must fallen years ago. Tall weeds grew among the collection of junk. The creaking building teetered and made a tiny moaning sound when an idle wind blew through it, as though it couldn't handle one more storm.

I wasn't about to park at the front of the house. My van could be easily spotted from the road. Skirting a huge rain-filled pothole, I drove slowly around to the back of the house, which had useless trash piled everywhere. I got out of the car and cautiously approached the broken back stoop, listening for any signs of life coming from within the house. I had never noticed how loud silence could be, how I could hear my blood rushing through my veins and the pounding of my heart like distant thunder. But that was all I heard.

I gathered up my courage and pushed the rotting back door open, its doorknob long gone. I stepped into a room that might have once been called a kitchen, and almost fainted from the stench that immediately assaulted me. I was going to throw up! I pulled a kleenex from my pocket and covered my nose and swallowed hard. Dear God, what could smell that bad? I took off the scarf from around my neck, draped it over the lower half of my face, knotted it in the back, and waited for the fabric combined with traces of my perfume to help filter the rotten air.

I gingerly stepped around the unrecognizable objects that littered the floor. As I walked into the next room, I discovered more stench. Several stained and ragged mattresses, filthy pillows, piles of soiled blankets, old newspapers — some in Spanish — beer cans, crumpled brown paper bags, a few playing cards, and more trash.

The doors between the the main part of the house and the two bedrooms had been removed, and one quick glance into the hovels sufficed. The condition of the bedrooms was no different than the rest of the place. A pigsty smelled better. I pushed my hand against my nose and found a second's relief from the fragrance that emanated from my scarf. But I hadn't seen everything yet. The worst was yet to come.

The stench was unmistakably that of human waste. I glanced through an open door, and clutched at my face again.

The bathroom was a sewer. The contents of a plugged-up toilet had emptied slimy water and clumps of hard feces onto the cracked linoleum floor. A gray, stained bathtub half hidden by the remnants of a shredded shower curtain sat accusingly against one wall, its bottom filled with human waste. I had never in my life seen such a…what?…hell? I had no words to describe such human neglect. This had nothing to do with poverty, this was…a man-made filth, degradation at its worst.

People had done this! What kind of people? I shuddered. I grabbed the bathroom door and pulled it shut with a bang. I had to get some air. I side-stepped the clutter on the floor with an odd kind of dance step and just before I reached the front door, I heard the sound of an approaching vehicle. My heart froze. My worst fears had come to pass. It had happened. I would have to talk my way out of this one.

I stepped to the side of the window, and with one finger moved the rag of a curtain just far enough to peek out. A black — oh my God — a black pickup truck was approaching the house. I could see two men in the front seat. Sammy and Willy? Mary had said the two killers drove a big black pickup. I broke out in a cold sweat. I was in trouble. Serious trouble! "Watch your back," Mary had said, "your life depends on it."

My mind raced.

I didn't have much time. I'd wait until they got out of the truck, and if they headed for the house I'd dash out the back and try to outrun them in my van. Fat chance of that. I was stuck in the loneliest place in the world, and trying to race away from two killers whose truck probably had a souped-up engine would be a one-sided affair. I wasn't exactly driving a Porsche. I watched the truck approach, my inside starting to quiver. I had really stuck out my neck.

The black truck rolled to a stop a few feet from the house, and I could see the faces of the two men under the wide brims of their cowboy hats. I remembered Mary's description: wide, broad face — Willy; narrow, sharp features — Sammy. The men in the truck were both talking at the same time, their expressions angry. The one in the driver's seat was gesticulating wildly with his hands, and suddenly smacked the steering wheel several times and yelled something at his partner. I could hear the sound of their voices, but could not make out the words.

The heated argument continued for a another moment, then the driver made a fist with his right hand and shook it in front of the other man's face, who ducked out of reach. The fist came down on the smaller man's shoulder, who did not respond, just turned his head and stared out the window.

The next thing I knew, the engine roared to life, the wheels turned sharply, and spewing mud and gravel, the truck bounced towards the silent country road at top speed, and turned north, away from town. I had not realized that I had been holding my breath while I waited for Sammy and Willy to come searching for me. My chest ached as I exhaled and gulped more foul air. I glanced around me for a minute or two. There was no doubt that Mexican illegals had been staying here. I didn't blame them for their wretched housing, for they were fugitive souls seeking a haven in the land of golden promise. God, I hoped they'd hold tightly to their long memories of shame and mistreatment and ask a bitter price for their misery when they found their voices to protest.

An urgency rose in me like an invisible red flag waving danger. Get out, get out, get out, the warning came. There was nothing here for me in this filthy, degraded place that I could connect to Mike. I wondered why Mary had suggested that I come here. Was it because I was being set up, and the only reason for the sudden departure of Willy and Sammy was because my van had not been visible, as it was parked at the rear of the house? With no vehicle in sight, no sign of the stranger snooping around, they had left. The more I thought about this idea, the more I was convinced that Sammy and Willy had been looking for me, and that Mary had been their source of information as well as mine. I felt no sense of guilt for thinking of Mary as an informer, a clever snitch who played both sides. I had never really been sure which side of the fence she was on, the sunny or the dark. You couldn't straddle the fence.

I had had enough of mental games, enough! I had enough. I was getting out of there.

I repeated my quick-step between the piles of trash and junk on the floor, held my breath until I got outside. Fresh air! I removed the scarf from my face, breathing deeply, sucking clean air into my lungs. I took off my jacket, shook it out, waved it back and forth into the wind like a flag, trying to get rid of the stink that clung to the fabric. I seriously doubted if I'd ever get the foulness of the farmhouse out of my memory.

Red, who was sitting in the passenger's seat of my van, greeted me with a friendly yelp. I patted my old buddy and gave him a big hug. I was grateful for his comforting presence. I was still in shock at what I had seen, and at the same time, I marveled at my luck of having been spared an encounter with Sammy and Willy. I didn't want to think just what the outcome might have been if they'd found me. As I headed toward the town, I worried if my luck was going to last, and decided it was high time to help my luck along. I knew what I had to do.

I wasn't going to spend another night in Chilton, Texas, and I was going to be especially vigilant for followers. The gang, the company, Mary, Sammy and Willy knew I was in town, staying in my dead brother's house. Alone. Talk about being a sitting duck!

It was late in the afternoon when I arrived at Mike's house, I checked the back yard for unexpected visitors, unlocked the front door and went into the house with Red preceding me. If there was a stranger in the house, he would let me know at once. He was a pretty good attack dog when

it came to protecting me. The house was empty and still. I
grabbed my overnight bag, packed my things in a hurry, and
in less than five minutes Red and I were back in the van and
heading for the highway that led west — west to home. I
said goodbye to no one. I just left.

On the outskirts of Chilton, I stopped for gas and
stocked up on snacks, drinks and sandwiches at the
adjoining mini market. I wasn't going to hang around cafés
and roadhouses. Was I watching my back? Yes, you bet I
was, Mary! I gazed in my rearview mirror when I turned
onto the highway to see if a black Ford pickup truck or any
other suspicious-looking vehicle was in sight. There was no
one behind me and traffic was light, which made driving a
lot easier. As soon as it grew dark I wouldn't be able to
make out the color of a vehicle, nor be able to determine its
make. Just like the German farmer said, "In the dark, all
cows are black."

The empty highway stretched out before me and I
mashed the accelerator with my foot and gathered speed. I
wanted to get as far away from Chilton as I could before
dark set in. I had about three more hours of daylight left.
That would bring me to a place I remembered where I could
spend the night. I wasn't going to take any chances. I'd have
traded in my vehicle for another car if I trusted anybody not
to tell about the trade. Also, I'd considered leaving my van
behind, flying home and asking Stewart to drive it to
Portland for me. I gave up on that idea quickly. Stew didn't
want to get involved or be asked for any favors.

I had calculated correctly the time and distance to the
small town where I wanted to stop for the night. The sky
had just lost its last touch of light when I pulled up in front
of Miller's Rest, a small, friendly-looking motel with white
plastic daisies in wooden window boxes. I checked in with

the round-faced, pink-cheeked, chatty Mrs. Miller and was given the room right next to the office. I asked her if she'd mind if I pulled my van around back. I explained that my vehicle had been broken into too many times, and I wanted it off the road and out of sight. She readily agreed, although in defense of her community, she assured me that break-ins just didn't happen at Miller's Rest. It was a right good neighborhood. When I signed in, I wrote down my residence as Nevada and assigned my vehicle a matching, fictitious license plate. Mrs. Miller never read my entry or saw the plate on my van parked in the rear.

After I carried my things into Unit One, I walked Red around for awhile, and then locked myself in my motel room for the night. I put my snacks on the table, filled Red's water bowl, gave him his dinner and turned out the lights. I pulled the one comfortable chair in front of the window and opened the curtains just enough for me to overlook the parking area in front of the motel. I wasn't going to sleep if I could help it. I would mount an overnight vigil. Red curled at my feet, and I settled in.

Time ticked away slowly, and whenever headlights approached the motel, I straightened up and peeked through the crack in the curtains to check on the vehicle and who got out. By one o'clock in the morning only one car had pulled in, an older man and woman who quietly moved into the room three doors down from mine. Soon, Mrs. Miller had switched off the big neon sign in front and the "No Vacancy" came on.

No one was coming after me. At least not now. Had I exaggerated the danger I was in? Had I gotten carried away with wild speculations? No, I didn't think so. Even though Mary seemed sincere and outwardly helpful, there were nasty secrets hidden in her head, to which I had no access.

She was quite a paradox. Here was a young, attractive woman whose bearing and looks alone could get her far, stuck in a dull, lonely Texas town working with high-level criminals, doing what, I didn't know. Assistant, pusher, delivery person, trouble shooter, partner, front person? What was her job? And why had she befriended me?

Somehow I didn't believe her confession of secretly carrying a torch for Mike. My brother may have been a nice guy, but he certainly wasn't the type who would appeal to her. She was elegant, he was country; she was sophisticated, he was simple; she was Armani, he was Levi. The differences were not the kind that attracted each other. It didn't wash. She was one clever lady, but I no longer believed she was innocent or without guilt.

I must have dozed off towards morning, when I felt Red's big head resting on my lap making his special sounds of greeting. I sat up with a start. Daylight was coming into my room through the split in the curtains and my watch told me it was seven o'clock. I had slept for several hours. The only other car in the parking area of the motel was a compact with Louisiana license plates. No black Ford pickup was in sight. I got myself ready for the rest of my journey, took Red for a walk, fed him breakfast, packed up my few things and went around back to my van.

Perhaps my departure from Chilton had gone unnoticed so far. But that it wouldn't last forever, and I had to keep my guard up. If Mary's bosses had plans for me, then the distance between Texas and Oregon would present no obstacle for them to get at me. I could go to the police at home with my suspicions, but I already knew their response: The police can't do anything unless a crime has been committed. If the crime were my dead body, they would have something to go on. Otherwise, no help.

I still had a twelve-hour drive ahead of me, and I was in a hurry.

The rest of my trip was uneventful. I was not followed and I started to relax a little. But I was not so foolish as to think I was free of Chilton, Texas. I was certain there would be another episode and in order to survive it, I would stay on my guard.

Chapter Eight

It was Friday morning, the kids were in school, Tom was asleep in bed following breakfast — three eggs sunnyside up, bacon, toast thickly spread with blackberry jam, and milk to drink — which he always looked forward to when he arrived home by 7:30 from his graveyard shift on the railroad crew, bucking cars for the Union Pacific.

Since my return from Texas, I doubt that we had exchanged ten civil words between us. I had experienced the silent treatment several times before, one of Tom's control strategies. Most of his methods to force his domination on me were ineffective. They never worked, but he kept trying. As for me, I enjoyed the period of quiet, aware that it would not last long, for Tom could not keep a damper on his resentment of me, his conviction, in this case, that he'd been grievously injured by my neglect of him while I was in Texas.

I gave him two days to nurse his sense of injustice into a peak of anger and frustration and then relieve the interior pressure by finding an excuse to blow up at me.

In the meantime, I enjoyed the peace before the storm. I sat in my bedroom office planning my next sales trip, glad that I had deliberately refused to occupy my mind with the violence, fear and disappointment I had encountered in Chilton.

I was not yet ready to make a final decision on the discoveries I had made in Texas or what to do with the deadly information I had collected. I certainly had no idea of how to judge its legal value, and knew I would have to consult someone with an expert knowledge of criminal law who could give me an opinion of how to proceed, or even if I should.

One big disappointment made me want to kick myself for carelessness and lack of foresight. The day after I returned to Gresham with my kids after the long haul from Texas, I drove to downtown Portland to the office of a forensic scientist. A woman named Cindy Day, who I had talked with on the phone, greeted me in her waiting room and invited me to join her in her personal office.

As we walked the short corridor walled on both sides with frosty glass, she noted my wrinkled nose and puzzled expression.

"You know," she smiled, "I forget that here we have our own special odors and chemical smells that come from tests we run on all sorts of material, organic and inorganic. You get used to strange odors. We've run analyses on fluids as complicated as the contents of a cow's stomach who died from something foreign she ate, to poisonous bread crumbs in which we located microscopic particles of aluminum. Deadly, of course."

I decided I liked this cheerful, honest woman. She sat herself in a comfortable chair behind her desk and indicated I should take the one that faced her.

I had debated with myself on just how much I should divulge to Dr. Day about the origin of the two vials I had brought back from Texas. Her friendly, comfortable and investigatory manner convinced me that she would not find my trips to Texas to investigate my brother's murder the journeys of a foolish woman, a woman who gave herself much more credit than she deserved for being able to uncover the facts that would lead to a verdict of homicide. Dr. Day accepted my short version of Mike's death and my Texas investigation with strong interest and not a hint of criticism, but she frowned when I laid the vials, which I had wrapped in kleenex, on her desk. Carefully, she pulled the kleenex free of the open bottles, and said, "From the condition of these bottles, I'm not hopeful. We'll try of course, but I don't want you to pin your hopes on a positive outcome. Too much wear and tear, I suspect."

When she telephoned me two days later with the bad news — too much contamination to make a positive identification that would hold up in court — I thanked her and said she could discard the bottles.

Of course, I was dejected by the outcome of the laboratory tests and as I sat in my office at home in a sort of moody daydream state, I thought how the results and consequences of the acts you perform in life take forever to come to a conclusion. Then I thought, what if they did take forever, what if I kept going and going and never reached a personal solution, but kept moving up into a darker darkness for all eternity…until I realized that the journey was God's judgment upon me?

For a moment deep fear ran through me and I felt terribly alone, isolated, out of touch with my surroundings, detached from my body as if I were dead, and I was absorbed with the question, why should I be condemned to eternal darkness? What have I done wrong with my life to deserve such a terrible fate? What have I done right? I asked.

I was a forty-two-year-old woman who had brought three children into the world, married a man I had come to hate and could count my few accomplishments on the fingers of one hand. My life, it seemed, could be summarized in losses. But then, as if my mind were a troubled sky, a thought like a sharp thread of lightning flashed against the darkness with the message: There is no gain, except by loss; there is no life, except by death; there is no vision except by faith.

I must have come out of my reverie, for contrary to the unease and futility I had experienced, now I felt rested and pleasantly whole as if I had done something unexpectedly fulfilling and worthwhile.

The next morning I was up early and left the house with Red at my heels for a long walk. Red loved the air when it was fresh after a rainy day, with the sun drying the wet ground and mist rising and catching rainbows from the golden light. We pranced along for two miles, then I decided it was time to turn back. As we neared my house, walking on the sidewalk on the opposite side of the street, my neighbor Becky came out to greet me.

There was a worry frown wrinkling her wide forehead and I asked what was troubling her. Forthright, never misleading, Becky looked me straight in the eyes and said, "The last two days there's been a man asking questions in the neighborhood. Looking for a woman who owns a dog named Red. Are you in trouble, Pam?"

My mouth turned dry and my heart leaped. I found it difficult to form the words that finally came from my lips, "What did he look like, Becky?"

"Like a Mexican, swarthy complexion, 'bout medium height and weight. Oh, yeah, he had a notch cut out of the top of his right ear, like a perfect v."

"Oh," I said and felt my stomach revolt in my throat. My mind flew back to the night at Harry's Texas Bar when Mary and I had talked and I had become fascinated with two Mexican women, dressed to kill in flashy clothes, parading across the room, drawing comments and lewd remarks from four men who sat across from us.

I stared at the smaller woman, vivid, attractive in a rich, sensual way, heavily made up with bright red lipstick and daubs of rose powder high on her cheeks. The taller woman wore a dark red silk dress that clung to her figure as if it had been painted on. Her petite, curvaceous companion, who was younger by six or seven years — probably she was about thirty or so — wore a striped blouse with the top buttons undone to reveal her luscious cleavage. A white canvas belt accentuated her tiny waist and a shiny black skirt clung to her hips and flared out as she walked.

Mary said, "The little pepperbelly, the younger one, has a temper like a firecracker. She took a hunk out of Chico's ear with a knife. He's sitting in the booth across from us with the three other guys."

"How did that happen?" I asked.

Mary could make her face unattractive with a smirky expression. Her lips curled back as she laughed with a nasty note of false admiration in her voice, "Her name's Conchita. At least that's what they call her. The story goes that Chico cornered her in the kitchen here where she works, and she sliced his ear with a butcher knife. It happened one afternoon when no one was in the bar and the cook had gone to the bathroom to relieve himself. He always took a magazine with him and was often gone for at least a half hour.

"She cut his ear because Chico was hurting her, forcing her back over the kitchen table, smothering her with his weight and not giving her a chance to complain, to tell him she wanted him to stop. Her fingers touched the knife on the table and, in that little moment of panic, as his hand went under her skirt and up between her legs, she raised the knife and sliced him on the ear twice, almost severing it. Later, she described his expression to some girlfriends and the story got around. She said he grabbed his ear with blood spurting out between his fingers, then wadded up a damp dish towel lying on a table and jammed it against the side of his face. She remembered saying — and thinking, 'I didn't mean to — You horny damn fool, I told you to stop. I didn't mean to hurt you so much.'

"Friends drove Chico to the hospital and they sewed his ear back on where it belonged, but a little perfect triangle of flesh was missing. Probably fell on the kitchen floor, or ended up in the hamburger beef, and Chico's ear healed with Conchita's love mark to remind him of her every time he combs his hair!"

The men in the booth across from us were close enough for me to get a good look at Chico, but we were too far away for me to see the cut in his right ear. His face was bold with a reckless cast to it and his black hair was swept straight back over his forehead. He looked dangerous.

Now, though, as I thanked Becky for her information about the dark-complexioned stranger who was canvassing our neighborhood for a woman who owned a dog named Red, the deep fear that had raised my adrenaline and prompted me to examine every lurking shadow while I was by myself in Chilton was back with sickening force, and I wondered how I'd protect myself.

The new nightmare lasted for two weeks, until one afternoon I heard a knock on my front door. I didn't have to look through the peephole to know, infallibly, that my visitor was Chico.

Of course, to affirm that my dread was not a false alarm, I walked quietly to the door and, hardly daring to breathe, pressed my right eye to the viewing hole and stared. One look convinced me. It was Chico all right, standing on my front steps bold and brazen. I marveled at his confidence. What had he expected of me? That I would open the door and politely invite him in for tea and a chat?

What in the hell was he after? I think I knew. I was positive I knew. It was Mike's ledger. They thought I had it. They had sent a messenger to retrieve it. He had come right up to my front door, I bet with no thought of immediate violence on his mind, to make a reasonable request, perhaps even to offer a reward for the incriminating ledger.

As I cautiously backed away from the door, I wondered how he would phrase it. "Ma'am, or Señora, you've got something we want. We don't want trouble. We don't want to hurt you, but we will if we have to. Just give me the ledger and you'll never see me again."

Chico lingered at the door maybe ten minutes, ringing the doorbell, making me nervous. When he finally left, I called the Troutdale Police Department and asked for Jack Collins. He was a real professional. I had visited with him earlier when the Gresham Police Department, our local protectors of the public, advised me impersonally that there was nothing they could do to protect me based on my unconfirmed fears.

I had called them on my final return from Texas, gave them a thumbnail sketch of what had happened in Chilton, and asked for advice. Nothing they could do, was their prompt answer, proving they didn't have to cogitate very long to reject my plea for help.

Jack Collins at Troutdale was a far different kind of cat. From the top of his wavy hair to the tips of his size sixteen shoes, he was all professional, all cop, with a brain that worked swiftly, a strong sense of protective guardian-ship for people his department served, and a contempt for members of his police brotherhood who believed their jobs were nine to five and required no special dedication.

He gave me a twenty-four-hour emergency number to contact him if Chico showed up again or in any way attempted to contact me or threaten me. I did spot Chico twice in the next two weeks and he followed me in his green van until I drove onto the Interstate, where I easily outdis-tanced him.

The third time I spotted Chico, my knees and legs turned to Jello. There was a companion riding in the seat next to Chico. I had seen the man once in the flesh, but the first time he stared at me with contempt and threat was in the dream that forced me out of bed to stand and shiver in the Idaho night. The nightmare turned out to be an accurate forecast of my brother's death, and it was he who had straddled Mike's back and held an airless plastic sack in place over his head until he shuddered and died of oxygen starvation.

I would never forget the killer's black bottomless eyes that drilled into me like burning coals.

I do not panic easily, but the day I saw Willy with Chico I was on the phone to Jack Collins immediately and described the man who killed my brother.

Jack asked me if I knew the man's name and whether I could describe him. I told Jack that the only name I knew was Willy. People always called him that. Then, I described Willy as a tall, muscular man whom I was certain worked out, pumped iron and was proud of his body. He had very strong hands, I added.

Jack asked me to wait on the line while he left the phone. When he came back, there was concern in his voice.

"We think this man is the same one who raped a thirteen-year-old in Troutdale about a year ago. He broke her nose, knocked out her front teeth, ruptured her spleen, cracked three ribs and broke both of her legs at the knees. He left her for dead in an Interstate motel. She lived to help a police artist make a composite of him. I want to send a copy over for you to identify. With your help, we may be able to take him off the streets. If he's the same man, his name is Willis Elmore and he's big trouble.

I didn't hesitate for a moment to identify Willy when a policeman rolled up in front of my house and came into my living room. The composite printout he showed me was Willy, without a question.

When the Troutdale policeman had left and I had locked the front door, I sat and remembered how Mary and I had sat in Harry's Texas Bar and she had told me some things about Willy — whom she said was the one who had asphyxiated Mike — that frightened her to recall.

Mary first met Willy at Harry's. He strolled in one night and saw her sitting by herself nursing a glass of iced tea with a lemon twist, a cube of sugar and a shot of vodka.

"What do you call that?" he asked.

"My own damn business," she replied, then realized he was not a man to be smart with, not with those evil, round, featureless, dark brown eyes like smudges from a burned-out fire. He stared down at her coldly from his six-foot-two height and seemed to swallow her, take her down into a cave inside himself where despicable creatures and formless nightmares with high insane laughs lived and mined the mud and filth for morsels of rotting flesh.

"Sorry," she apologized and let her breath out slowly, afraid to make a sighing noise that might alert him to how frightened she was. Of course, she did not protest when he slid into the booth beside her, a massive bulk so thick through the chest that he had to push the table to give himself clearance to sit comfortably.

Their conversation, Mary told me, was both elemental and terrifying to her because he quickly let her know that he had seen her in the past perform in a Dallas strip club.

"Yeah," Mary said to me, "It's a phase of my life I'm not proud of. I supported myself through Southern Methodist U showing my knockers to the guys who yelled and hollered every time I took off my bra and twirled it in the air."

Sitting next to Mary, Willy had a good profile of her breasts and he said to her, "Yeah, I remember you." He paused, grinned and stared pointedly at her chest. "I never forget great knockers. You should be proud."

"Thanks," she said.

Then for no reason Mary could think of, for she certainly had not encouraged him, he started describing his life before he came to Chilton as a specialist. Curious as to what a specialist did, Mary almost blurted out the question but caught herself in time. She decided she didn't want to know.

But Willy was not reticent about his job. "We both work for the same outfit," he said, "so there's no need for secrets. I clean things up, whatever it takes. Yeah," he laughed, "Mr. Clean, that's me."

He explained to Mary that his cleanup jobs often required "attitude adjustments" and if that didn't work, then he would use more drastic measures. They often proved fatal to the offenders, he said.

That's when he started reminiscing about his professional career, as he called it, starting with his first robbery when he was sixteen. That was in Killeen, Texas, near Fort Hood, when he stalked two army boys fresh from the paymaster. He took ninety-seven dollars from them and sent them both to the hospital, one with a skull fracture.

He was a Texan by birth, home town Marshall in East Texas where he had worked, after he dropped out of high school, in the oil fields that sprouted towering rigs like dandelions out of the sandy soil.

He had a baby face, Willy, but as Mary observed to herself, he was built like a gorilla and it didn't take much imagination to spot the mean streak that ran through him — it showed in his cold, burnt-cinnamon eyes with the flat look they took on when he was displeased.

Mary was more than a little afraid of Willy, not only because she was certain that he was unstable, but because he had made it plain that he wanted to get into her pants. His admiring crack about her knockers had been his opening gambit and she shuddered at the idea of being handled by him.

She also knew that if he pursued her she wouldn't have a choice but to give in. There was a dogged strength of will in him that brooked no resistance. She was as certain as her own name that Willy had injured women, had even enjoyed making them cringe with terror, pacified them with assurances and when they thought they were safe, pounced on them like a wolf on a rabbit.

Mary was not surprised to learn through the Chilton grapevine that it was Willy and his partner, Sammy, who had killed Mike Penrose.

Chico and Willy disappeared and though I was vigilant for six more weeks, taking extraordinary precautions, never placing myself in a vulnerable position where I could be overcome and thrown into a fast car, I still woke up apprehensive and jittery. I jumped when stationary shadows moved or noises occurred where I thought they should never be. But gradually, I began to feel safer, and slowly, I developed a philosophy that did not comfort my inadequacy for failing to identify Mike's killers, but did give me a viewpoint about murder that helped bring an end to my deep anger. I came to see that a murderer sets himself aside from all of humanity forever. It is a real death of the self. I thought about Sammy and Willy, men who conspired in their own dying long before their hearts stopped beating. And I did not feel sorry for them.

Notwithstanding my returning sense of security from threat or attack, I was certainly not convinced that reverberations from my Texas episode were at an end. I hoped I was wrong.

Chapter Nine

Spring in Oregon is a magical time. Everything that pokes out of the earth blossoms and blooms. Winter-dry trees fill their bare limbs with showers of luscious leaves, green, while others burst out in vivid colors that dazzle the eye. It is always new, fresh and beautiful, like a promise.

I sat in my office looking out of the window at the flowers displayed in my garden, and I felt old, tired and ugly. Earlier, I had endured Tom's criticisms about the way I cooked meals, moved chairs and combed my hair.

It had become my habit, when Tom scolded or screamed, to escape to my office and lock the door behind me.

Almost seven months had passed since we buried Mike, and my clumsy attempts at solving his murder had brought no results. The visits from Chico and Willy had stopped long ago. But, at least I had proved to my family that Mike did not commit suicide. That's all I was certain of

— not that it lessened the pain of his loss. He was dead, and that hurt.

Even though my company had promoted me to district manager, I was still traveling a great deal. However, being on the road was not a hardship for me and I acknowledged it. I used my work as an escape. It got me out of the house. I was running away from home. I was dodging the problems of my marriage by physically removing myself from the scene, which of course solved nothing. You can't run and hide forever and turn your back to the truth. One day I would have to come out of hiding.

I always took the children along on my business trips, since I didn't trust them to the care of their father. During school days, Adam stayed with my mother, who had recently moved to Gresham. Nathan and Kathleen went with me. If Tom abused the kids with ugly words and occasional beatings when I was present, there was no telling what he would do if I left him alone with them.

I hoped he would change one day. Maybe I would discover some magical ways to please my husband; I would change him. Sure, I'd fix me first and that in turn would fix him. That was the way I thought then. I was a woman of responsibility, determination and stick-to-it-iveness. I wouldn't give up on my husband. I'd hang on to our marriage like a dog with a bone. I knew I could make our union work. I could fix anything.

I maintained my positive attitude, even though I had discovered evidence that my husband had slept with another women in our bed during one of my sales trips. Of course he denied it. In the end he convinced me that the tell-tale signs of lovemaking — used condoms — that he carelessly left for anyone to find, had been ours. Of course he was lying, but apparently I must have found it more comforting to go along with him. What was the alternative? Leave him? Oh, we'd talked about it. Talked about it often. But I was still around, wasn't I?

In my fury, I spent my anger on sanitizing the bedroom. I tore up the bedding, scrubbed the headboard bookcase and cleaned and vacuumed the room thoroughly. Barely able to touch the sheets and towels, I dumped them in the washing machine, added an extra shot of bleach and when they emerged fresh and fragrant from the dryer, I made up the bed and put the fluffy towels back into the bathroom. All I'd cleaned was the exterior veneer of my life; my spirit needed rehabilitation just as badly.

On the rare occasions that we had sex, Tom had become abusive and ugly. The act was more rape than joyful physical union. I didn't understand where he had acquired his new and despicable habits during the act: hitting me, handling me roughly, abusing me with dirty words. I wondered who had taught him to do this. I did put a stop to it with one effective blow to his genitals. He groaned and rolled out of the bed onto the floor, clutching himself in pain. That was the end of that.

But he was bent on embarrassing me at every opportunity. On one occasion when two friends of mine were visiting me for a few days, he came up to me in the kitchen while they were seated at the breakfast table, grabbed my crotch and insisted that we go upstairs and f.... I was embarrassed to tears; I was mortified, insulted and disgusted. I ran from the room.

I did a lot of that, running to avoid his campaign of deprecating me. But always I returned, coming back for more. I made every effort to please him. When he took up gambling, I gambled along with him until his wagering drove us to the brink of bankruptcy.

It was the sixteenth year of our marriage on a rainy day in early spring. The children were playing in the house, Tom was taking a nap, and I was doing some pleasant, diverting paperwork in my office at home. I had returned from a selling trip the night before, and was dressed in beat-up old jeans and a bulky sweater.

Nathan and Kathleen were at the kitchen table with their coloring books. When I went to freshen my coffee cup, I was pleased with their sporadic laughter and giggles peppered with occasional moments of sibling bickering. The kids were having a good time. The house was peaceful. I had cleaned and straightened up the downstairs earlier in the morning. Everything was neat, everything was in its place. I had even made preparations for dinner. We were going to have Tom's favorite meal, pot roast, vegetables, roasted potatoes, a green salad and an All-American apple pie.

Just then my husband appeared, wearing his favorite grubby jeans and an old T-shirt. He got out of bed about the same time as I did on the days he worked eight to five. However, one look at his angry face warned me that he was about to pick a subject upon which to launch an argument. His appetite for violence never seemed to dissipate.

As always, his eyes glittered with a reddish glow when he started to rage. His face turned to stone, his jaw granite-like. The set of his shoulders was rigid, stubborn and ungiving. His lips twisted and distorted as though the foul words pouring from his mouth etched their passage in lines of malevolence.

"Who in the hell made that goddam noise that woke me up," he demanded in a deceptively normal voice, looking angrily at Nathan, whose lower lip was quivering. Tom's arm shot out then, and he shook the little boy like a bag of bones.

"Kathleen and I were just having fun," Nathan cried, trying to avoid the blows that rained on his head and face. He held his hands over his cheeks protectively as though to stop the angry red marks from his father's blows. His eyes reflected his fear and he sobbed pitifully. I jumped across the room and landed a sharp blow on Tom's face that sounded like wood cracking. Nathan used the diversion to tear out of his father's grip.

I held on tightly to the terrified child, soothing him, loving him and shouting at his father. In my anger, my vocabulary was no better than the filth that came out of Tom's mouth when he was mad.

Tom howled when I attacked him. Spittle formed in the corners of his mouth, as he grabbed for Nathan again. "That little son-of-a-bitch is going to learn to be quiet when I rest," he shouted. "And you, you f... bitch, you're too fat and too goddam lazy to keep them quiet. And," he added, sticking out his chin at me, "you're too stupid to know what's good for you, you whore." He tried to get at Nathan again, but I quickly turned my back on him, reached for Kathleen — who was clinging to my leg petrified, and had started to cry — with my free hand, took the kids with me to my bedroom and locked the door behind us. Tom stopped his tirade, but I knew he was seething. Another battle, but there were no winners in our ugly games.

I held and loved the children for a long while. We talked, and I read them stories. They were as exhausted as I was. I put Kathleen down for a nap, and Nathan went to his room, where he curled up on his bed with some picture books and his favorite bear. I kept going back and forth between my bedroom and the childrens', talking softly to them, loving them. I knew they would fall asleep. I told Nathan I was going to take a bath, and then rest for awhile.

I left his room and gently closed the door. I would check on them after I had my bath.

I locked myself in the bathroom, ran a hot tub and dropped some bath oil in the water. I hastily stripped off my clothes, wishing I could wipe from my mouth the bitterness and ugliness of the scene that had played out in the kitchen.

Gratefully, I sank into the warm, scented water and tried to erase the fight we had just had. I didn't want to remember his rigid jaw, his embittered face, and the insults that fell from his lips like acid rain.

Nothing had changed since we had had our last fight. But what in the world had I expected? He was the same man, with the same attitudes, views and temper. I was the same woman expecting him to have changed miraculously overnight. What a merry-go-round I was on. I closed my eyes, weary, worried, unsure of myself and everything else in my life. But more than that, I felt unloved, alone and lost. I remembered a popular Broadway play and I slowly mouthed the title, "Stop the world, I want to get off!"

Suddenly, with my black mood still dominant, I felt a strange warmth radiating in the air that did not emanate from the hot water in the tub. I opened my eyes slowly, and to my amazement the small bathroom was illuminated with the same bluish-white light that had visited me more than twenty years ago. And, just like that time, a form emerged from its center and floated towards me. This time, the figure was not hidden from view by a hooded cloak, and a face was revealed to me. It was a human face, but the expression on it far transcended any words that I could possibly use to describe its magnificent, ethereal beauty and a calm that conveyed immeasurable love and peace.

I was in awe. I was in the presence of Eternity.

The light grew stronger, and in my head I heard a soft voice asking me to hold out my hands. I turned sideways in the tub, stretching my arms, water dripping onto the floor, toward the Light. The figure took both of my hands within the folds of her energy. I felt no physical pressure of being touched, but that same healing warmth my spirit remembered spread through all of my being. It was a blissful, overwhelming rapture. Everything I had ever feared, all the pain I had accumulated in my heart, all my feelings of loneliness and despair, the insults and the abuse — everything — fell away in that one blessed moment.

The gentle voice in my head whispered, "Remember this moment. You are loved. Remember, you are loved."

I wanted to hold on to the Light forever, but the beautiful face faded back into the blue-white mass of energy, which became brighter and stronger for a moment. Energy, Love, Peace, Comfort and Bliss. Energy. I repeated those five powerful words and wanted to mold them into armor for my spirit, my protection forever. I was a little desperate to hold on to my vision, make it grow stronger and me wiser because of it. I was fortunate; I felt blessed to have had the experience. My deep feeling of being lost and lonely had vanished and been replaced with an infallible knowledge of being loved.

I slid back into the warm water and rested my back against one side of the tub, still feeling the comfort and peace of the Blue Lady's presence. I pondered her words, "You are loved. Remember this moment. You are loved."

Isn't that what life is all about? I asked myself. Loving a child or adult, male or female, cat or dog, everyone's well-being was based on being loved. Things and stuff, belongings and prestige, sex and status had nothing to do with love. Love was the respect and gratitude with which we celebrated other human beings, and especially, ourselves. How could we expect to be loved when we didn't know how to love ourselves? Grateful for the astonishing insight, I had an inkling I would make it.

Evening came and I had dinner with the children. Tom had left and missed out on my All-American meal. What the hell, he would probably have found fault with it anyway. The kids were quiet and subdued, as they always were after the storm of their father's fury had passed, leaving all of us bruised and battered. After I tucked them in for the night, I read stories to them until they fell asleep. I went to bed, pulled the blankets around me, wrapped my heart and soul in the memory of the Blue Light, and went to sleep, peacefully, blissfully. If and when Tom came home he would have to sleep on the living room couch. He claimed my presence in the bed made it uncomfortable for him. So be it.

The appearance of my — what? — guardian angel, the Blue Lady, Mother of Mercy, whoever — stayed with me. It insulated me against Tom's nastiness, protected me from his foul words and obscene gestures and helped me love my children even more.

The next day, I went back on the road. I had some traveling to do for my company. Business was good but the song we endured at home had the same old refrain: Tom loved my paychecks, but complained bitterly about my absences during the week. I was gone for three days, and when the children and I returned all hell broke loose. Again!

I had picked up Adam from my mother, parked the van in the garage, let Red in the backyard, settled the children in their rooms, and unpacked my things. I had changed into a comfortable, faded old blue sweat suit and a pair of soft sneakers, tied my hair back in a ponytail, and gone to the kitchen to fix a snack. A few moments later, Tom walked in.

He had been out, who knows where. He shoved his hands into his pants pockets, rocked back on forth on his heels for a while, criticizing me with his eyes.

He stood rocking on his heels and staring at me in deadly silence. Not a good sign! I looked up and saw his lips curled into a malicious sneer. "You look like crap! Where in the hell did you dig up that outfit? You couldn't give it away on the street. A bag lady has better taste in clothes than you. You're really letting yourself go, you dumb bitch, you're looking like hell!"

With one quick motion, he stepped in front of me, blocking my way, and began his normal song and dance — ranting and raving. His voice assumed the malicious tone of threat and fury.

"Just look at you," he shouted, "Don't you ever look in the mirror, you bitch? Can't you see you're getting fat and ugly? You know I hate fat people, and you keep doing it to me. You're getting fatter every day! Your hair is a mess, your clothes are crap, and you don't care...you..."

I put down my cup quietly, turned sideways to get around him, but he grabbed the folds of my sweat suit around my neck, and jerked me back to where I had stood in front of him. He held me in his iron grip and his ugly words rained on my heart. I had heard it all before. I hated him. No, cut that out! I loved him, didn't I? I turned my head away from his distorted face, and looked out the kitchen window at the dark sky. I thought I could hear the wind rush through the trees and wanted to follow it into the night.

Enough! I had to stop this madness before the children were sucked into Tom's wrath. So I started to yell back, raised my arms, clenched my hands tightly into fists, beat against his chest until I had managed to push myself away from him. With his foul words following me out of the kitchen, I ran upstairs and locked myself in my bedroom. I was exhausted, filled to the brim with my own measure of fury and despair.

Out of breath, I stood in the middle of the room, shaking and shouting senseless rebukes and words of anger, when all of a sudden, out of nowhere, the blue-white Light appeared a few feet away from me. For a second or two, I stood motionless as I watched the figure of a beautiful human emerge from its center just as had happened twice before. With the hot anger still boiling within me, I put my hands on my hips and challenged the Light. I shouted, "What are you doing here? What do you want? What am I doing so wrong?"

I became still, and heard a gentle voice say to me, "You're mad, blaming Tom for your troubles."

Still with my hands defiantly resting on my hips, like a housewife squabbling with a quarrelsome neighbor across the fence, I replied, "How dare he treat me like this. I am a good person. I love him! Why can't he love me? How dare he?"

The figure moved what looked like an arm of energy and light toward me and in a comforting voice, said, "How dare You? You're loving him with strings attached. You want him to be something he can never be. Who's driving whom crazy? You're causing your own grief."

Dear God! I stood there in my bedroom exchanging words with an incredible, out-of-this-world apparition, and I was arguing. I was hearing a truth I had never considered before. I was shocked. I wanted the Light to side with me.

The voice grew stronger as it repeated, "Remember, you are causing your own grief. He cannot be what you want him to be. Furthermore, you have nothing to do with his anger. Let go.

"Now tell him I have appeared, and what I've said to you is my message for him as well."

With a soft and gentle motion, and soundlessly, the image floated away, blended into the Light and grew more brilliant for a split second. The Light spread a feeling of warmth, comfort and love around me, then faded until there was no glimmer left, and the room was as dark as the night outside my window.

I didn't move for the longest time, and stayed glued to the spot. My body was relaxed, my hands had fallen by my sides, and my heart was at peace. What had I just learned? Why hadn't I thought of those simple words before? Surely, I must have felt them. Why had I evaded the truth? Had my stubbornness to "see things through or die" blocked out all logic and robbed me of rationally appraising my life? I didn't have the answers for what had been, but now, I had the answer to what would have to be.

I took off my old sweat suit, dressed in a pair of good pants and a silk shirt — not for Tom, but for me. I stepped into the bathroom, combed my hair, touched up my makeup a little, and slowly went downstairs looking for my husband. I found him in his favorite chair watching television.

Without saying a word, I walked in front of him, turned off the television set, and faced him. He first registered surprise as he saw me well-dressed, but just a second later, storm clouds gathered in his eyes in answer to my act with the T.V. Without apology, I stretched out my arms, palms up, like a cop directing traffic, and before he could say anything, I quickly told him about the Light, and the Blue Lady. My voice remained firm and must have contained enough authority for him not to interrupt.

"This is the third time she has appeared to me," I explained quietly. "I don't question who she or he is. All I know is that the vision is real, it has helped me to understand myself. Here is the message I am supposed to bring to you. First, let me tell you that I am sorry that I have loved you with strings attached. I have loved you expecting your love in return. I wanted you to be the kind of person you just can't be. I am sorry. I am not blaming you. I am ready to let go of you. I have also learned that I am not responsible for your anger. That is yours to handle. And," I concluded softly, "there will be a loving change." I stopped, never taking my eyes off of his face.

Tom didn't say anything for a minute and appeared a bit shocked and surprised at what I had just told him. When he finally replied, he shook his head from side to side, got to his feet, uttered a curt, "You're nuts," under his breath, and walked away. I looked at his broad shoulders as he disappeared through the front door, and took it as a sign that he not only had walked out of the room, but out of my life as well.

Even though Tom dismissed what I said with those two careless words that translated into "I don't believe it," something must have reached him which he was unable or unwilling to admit. Something happened. Something wonderful.

He never touched the children again. He never subjected them to one of his cruel tongue lashings again. I was grateful for that, but nothing had changed in his attitude and behavior towards me. Where I was concerned, he had his control and emotional abuse pattern down to a science, and practiced both of them religiously. But things had changed for me. I no longer expected his love. I was no longer hurt and disappointed. He was the way he was. I accepted that.

And, the words that came from my vision... "there will be a loving change" ... never left my mind. I had become much more at peace with myself. At quiet moments, and at times when I was behind the wheel of my van, I took time out to examine myself. I found "me" to be a nice person who needed to be loved by no other than myself. I would have to learn to appreciate myself, to understand that I deserved the gifts my Creator had bestowed on me at the moment of my birth. I had a lot to learn.

The following week I was working in Portland, and just after I settled down to write some letters in my home office, the telephone rang. As I picked up the receiver, I felt a brief sense of warning wash over me, and I wasn't at all surprised when the voice on the other end turned out to be that of Mary from Texas.

After a brief and hurried greeting, Mary's said to me in a rush, "I called to tell you something you need to know, and," she emphasized with her demanding authority, "I want you to do something about it. I'm at Barry's Holmen's house, You met him at Mike's funeral. Remember? He was a good friend of your brother's."

Sure, I remembered him. He was a tall, husky man, with sandy-colored hair and clean-shaven face with merry, gray eyes set wide apart. He had an infectious grin that invited you to laugh with him. He seemed a gentle and jolly fellow. I had no idea he had been working for the same gang that had snared Mike.

"He's dead," Mary rambled on. "He's hanging from a rafter in his garage. He's been murdered just like Mike. The body is still warm, and if you call the police now and give them the address, they can come out here and get a handle on it."

"Wait a minute! Just a minute!" I interrupted, raising my voice. I was shaken and confused, trying to catch my breath and squelch the awful sensation of hot terror rising in my throat. Mike's limp body dangling grotesquely from his cherry picker flashed before my eyes. Oh, God! It had happened again. What would stop these killers?

Before I could voice another protest or ask a question, Mary said, "Barry was murdered, It's the same m.o. as Mike's. He was killed somewhere, brought back to his house, and then strung up. The killing has all the marks of a Willy and Sammy job. Only this time, the boys must have been in an awful hurry to get away. The ladder is lying on the floor, more than ten feet away from the spot where Barry is hanging. He couldn't possibly have used it," she said, then she seemed to lose control — a rather unusual thing to happen to Chilton Mary.

"Please," she urged, her voice firmer, "call the Chilton police and tell them Barry Holmen is dead. He's hanging in his garage at 145 Carriage Way. He's hanging from a rafter, and the body's still warm. I've got to run now. I can't afford to be seen by anybody. The police know who you are, and perhaps they'll believe now that Mike was murdered when they see Barry — dead, just like Mike. Well, I don't know, it might help you." She broke the connection with the inference that she would call back later.

For a moment, I stared at the silent receiver in my hand, and then replaced it slowly in its cradle. Well, I had quite a few things to digest. First, poor man! Barry had seemed to be a such a neat guy. Another innocent had lost his life, for what? Money? A few extra bucks? That's what it boiled down to. It was always all about money. That's what I couldn't understand about Mike. Was he so dumb as not to know that there was no free lunch? Did he bother at all to check on his principal benefactor, who had so readily financed him into his own business? Didn't my brother know that he'd owe somebody dearly for handing him a jackpot opportunity?

The next piece in the puzzle, of course, was Mary. Who in the hell was she? Friend or foe? Gang member or informer, double agent, a rotten apple? Surely that. God knows what else. Why would she call me to report another death to the police in Chilton? She could have made an anonymous call from any pay phone wherever she was. Why did she want to involve me? I had been followed, I had been stalked, my life had been in danger, and Mary had been my contact. Always, she had been the go-between. What was her real motive in sucking me into another homicide? There was no end to the puzzle she represented. I was convinced that Mike's death, and perhaps Barry's murder, would remain just an unsolved crime.

I picked up the phone and called the Chilton Police Department. Not because of Mary's instruction, but for something I knew I had to do.

The officer who answered the telephone in Chilton, Texas at police headquarters told me stay on the line. He'd get Sergeant Myers who was familiar with the Penrose case.

I remembered Sergeant Myers; he wasn't the one who had insulted me. When he came on the line, I quickly told him about my phone call from Mary. I dutifully relayed the news of Barry Holmen's death, who, according to my informant, I said, had met his death under circumstances identical to my brother's. I gave him the dead man's address.

The police sergeant listened patiently on the other

end. "I'll send my best men out there right now. Hang on,
I'll be right back." I could hear the click of the hold button
as he left the line.

"Here I am again," he announced cheerfully a moment
later. "My boys are on their way to the Holmen house.
They'll call me as soon as they are on the scene, and if you
and I are still talking on the phone, I'll tell you what they
found. In the meantime," he added in a fatherly fashion a la
Texas, "Don't you worry your pretty little head about that,
now."

I had done some quick and thorough thinking in my
pretty little head before I made the call. I had been
drawing on strength from the depth of an unknown
reservoir in me, and had made a momentous decision. And
it felt good.

"Sergeant. Myers", I said, "let me tell you something.
I don't need to know what happened to Barry Holmen. I
don't need to hear any more lies, or truths for that matter,
about my brother's death. I'm through. I'm all through. I'm
letting go. I'll be sending you all the papers and the few
notes I have accumulated in my attempt to solve Mike's
murder. I'll send you everything I have, and I don't ever
want to be contacted again by anybody from Chilton, Texas.

"My brother didn't have sense enough to recognize
trouble when it looked him in the face, and he got himself
killed. Regardless of your department's findings, other
people's opinions or recommendations, my brother did not
commit suicide. I dreamt his murder weeks before it
happened. I know that's neither relevant nor believable. But
it's the truth, if that matters. The fact remains, I didn't need
a degree in forensics or criminology to determine that Mike
was murdered.

"Now, I'm through with it. I'll do no more! Thank you

for listening to me, and please don't contact me again. I won't talk to you."

I hung up.

I sat quietly for a long time looking out into the garden. I listened to the drip-drop of the soft spring rain landing on the thick rhododendron leaves. The tulips had closed their petals against the grey skies and the rain. Only bright sunshine could coax them to open up again. I was closing up too. I remembered what Mike had said a long time ago. It may even have been a line from a song he liked. I could hear the sound of his voice in my head: "Baby, the sun will shine, but first the rain must fall."

Two hours later, my phone rang. It was Mary — the last person in the world to whom I wished to talk.

"Say, Pam," she said, after a brief greeting, explaining she just had to see how I was, "I heard you are giving up all efforts to investigate Mike's death any further. I heard you were through. What brought that on? Is it true?"

"Yep! It's true," I answered. "And," I added with a saccharin tone of voice, "that goes for you too. Never call again! I don't trust you, nor do I understand your motives, but I don't think they benefit me. I'm getting on with my life. Thanks, if you think you deserve it!"

I hung up the phone.

What in the hell was she all about? I congratulated myself for breaking the connection with her. I did puzzle about how she knew what I had told the police sergeant in Chilton. On whose team was she playing? I had asked myself that once before, and I did not come up with a satisfactory answer then either. Had her news about the death of Mike's friend been another bait to get me involved once more in Mike's death? did "they" — she, Willy and

Sammy — think that I would rush back to Chilton and play Sherlock Holmes again, placing myself in a final jeopardy?

I was through. For a long time, my life and Mike's had run parallel. We had both been traveling on a path of self-destruction that led to a dead end. It was too late for Mike, but it wasn't too late for me. I had chosen another path — the road to an expanded life!

I wanted to celebrate. I wanted to do something that was symbolic of the way I felt. So, I got in my van, drove to the nearest nursery, looked at all the lovely greeneries that were aching for a garden in which to grow, and finally chose a young, pink-blossomed tulip tree. The nursery man gave me instructions for planting, and I put the tree in my van and drove home.

Before I carried my new little friend into the backyard, I went into my office to retrieve the roll of film John Webb had taken at the scene of Mike's death. It had never been developed and had never left my possession except for the short interval it was in my father's hands. I carried the tulip tree to the backyard along with my big shovel. I dug a deep hole at a spot near my office window, and dropped the roll of film into the dark soil at the bottom. After I filled the hole halfway with water, I planted the sapling, covering its roots with soil so it could grow and blossom. It would be my constant reminder of the abundant gifts the universe bestows on us, and a sign to remind me to celebrate the renewal of life.

Epilogue

I did not solve the murder of my brother. My feeble attempts, my inexperience in criminal matters and the amateurish manner with which I approached the problem did not bring about the demise of the powerful criminal empire responsible for Mike Penrose's murder and the deaths of others. The lords of crime remain ensconced in their palaces of evil and continue to dispense death and misery from their gilded thrones, secure and arrogant.

But I let go of it. I broke free of the responsibility I had taken upon myself to avenge my brother's death. And that felt good.

I did not leave my husband, Tom, for another three years. With the same tenacity with which I searched for the truth in Mike's death, I pursued my pipe dream of having a happy marriage. After all, I was such a good person, wasn't I?

But I let go of that eventually. I broke free of the responsibility of filling another human heart with love, when the heart was empty. Whatever love I stuffed into Tom's heart escaped, vented by his anger and deep insecurity. I let him go, and that felt good.

I am pleased with what breaking free has given me. I am thrilled about having discovered the secret of letting go. It may not be a big secret to some people, but it was for me, and it is very much like the following classic story someone once told me. I didn't really understand it then. But I do now!

The mighty gods and goddesses of antiquity had gathered in their celestial realm and created man (woman). They created man in their collective images and bestowed upon him all but one gift they themselves possessed. They gave him an eye for beauty, an ear for the truth, a taste for life, emotions to love and cherish others, and talents too bountiful to recite.

But they did not bestow "Genius" on him. That, they argued, would make him god-like. So, they decided to hide that god-like quality from him and debated where to hide it. They didn't want to hide it on the lofty heights of a mountain, nor on the bottom of the deepest ocean. Eventually, they concluded in harmony, man would find it there.

So the gods and goddesses hid the gift of Genius within man. They knew he'd never look for it there.

I searched for love and acceptance from others, and came up empty-handed. But when I looked inside of me, and discovered my self worth and began to appreciate and love myself, I was indeed breaking free. I learned that I did not have to prove my worth to the world, and learned to trust myself.

When I realized that I deserved the best life has to offer, that I was qualified to be respected and loved, to live in peace with a tranquil heart, it was then that I asked Tom to leave. There's no reason in the world that any human being has to live with abuse, and lack of respect and dignity.

My children had to unlearn their father's ways and have learned to treat me with respect, as I treat them. Our little family has pulled together in harmony and peace. Growing up is a painful task, we all have to do it, but it's a lot easier when we learn to love ourselves.

All our Godly gifts are hiding within. All we have to do is to break free.

May it happen to you. You deserve it.

Pamela Penrose

To order additional copies of

Breaking Free

Book: $15.00   Shipping/Handling $3.50

Contact: ***BookPartners, Inc.***
P.O. Box 922, Wilsonville, OR 97070
Fax: 503-682-8684
Phone 503-682-9821
Phone: 1-800-895-7323